REASON FOR LIVING

A Burn Survivor's Story of Hope and Rebirth

By

George E. Pessotti

OUR AMERICAN JOURNEYS
Amherst, Massachusetts

Distributed by Applewood Books
Bedford, Massachusetts

ISBN: 1-55709-052-1

Thank you for purchasing an Our American Journeys book.
Our American Journeys is a division of Our Publishing Company,
PO Box 3561, Amherst, MA 01004

Our American Journeys helps people with stories to tell publish their story.
Through a program of self-sponsored publishing, this innovative project
brings into print—and provides a forum for sales and marketing—journals,
diaries, personal accounts, and memoirs.

Our American Journeys books are distributed by
Applewood Books, PO Box 365, Bedford, MA 01730.

For more information about Our American Journeys, its authors and titles,
visit us on the web at www.OurAmericanJourneys.com.

I dedicate this book to my Mom, Dad,
Joanne, Stephen, David, family and friends.
You taught me the meaning of unconditional love.

FOREWORD

The Phoenix Society for Burn Survivors was founded with a vision that those who had experienced a burn injury have a wealth of knowledge and the ability to positively impact the lives of those who find themselves impacted by burn trauma. In other words, no one should have to go it alone. George Pessotti embodies that vision.

When he was hospitalized with burn injuries in 1979, George was visited by the founder of the Society, Alan Breslau. Since that memorable visit, George has taken the powerful lessons he learned that day and used them to help thousands of others. He has served as a volunteer, mentor, donor, trustee and even the interim Executive Director of The Phoenix Society over the past 25 years. He continues to be a passionate champion for the work of the organization.

In the New England area George works tirelessly making personal visits to the burn centers to connect with new survivors and families just like Alan did for him. He also facilitates a support group, assists with finding burn care experts for those in need, and organizes many fundraising events, all while working full time as a estate planner and independent broker. His work has not stopped at the local level.

George has played a major role in shaping The Phoenix Society and positioning it as the world leader in peer-based recovery services for those impacted by a burn injury. His dedication to fund development for the organization has played a particularly important role in our success. He understands that without adequate resources we cannot achieve our vision. He has raised well over $150,000 in just one of his events, the Paul Noel Memorial Golf Tournament. George is an avid golfer, so this event allowed him to combine two of his life passions. Since his initial event he has added several other events and helped to develop our major giving program.

The funding raised by his efforts helped to establish our website, which connects thousands searching for help to available resources and access to peer support. Our newest program, SOAR (Survivors Offering Assistance in Recovery), is a formal program offered in over 20 burn centers that now assures that families have access to someone who has been there and can share the hope of life after burn trauma. The program most dear to George's heart is the annual World Burn Congress, where hundreds of survivors come together to learn and grow from their mutual experiences. He has personally funded hundreds of survivors to attend this life-changing event and has been a strong support mentor to those who seek him out for support during the Congress. I do not think George realizes how many lives he has touched over the years both directly and indirectly through his efforts. The gifts I most treasure about George as a friend and fellow burn survivor are his love of life and his ability to see the humor in our travels through life. I have no doubt that the pages of his book will bring to light his many gifts.

Amy Acton
Executive Director
The Phoenix Society for Burn Survivors, Inc.
www.phoenix-society.org

PROLOGUE

Cats are said to have nine lives. Having narrowly escaped death three times, I have often hoped that human beings have the same allotment. But what if that's wrong? Could I already be on my last life? The thought prompts me to make sure my story gets told before my time runs out.

Over the years, dozens of people who have heard about what happened to me in 1979, when I was 31, have had the same response: "That's a heck of story, George. That you survived all of that is very inspirational. You should write a book; I'd like to read it."

Most of these people didn't know that I already had written that book; I began writing it near the end of the approximately two years' worth of events recounted here. Having been encouraged to keep a diary as a way to help relieve the emotional stress I was experiencing at that time, I instead had chosen to put my writing into the form of a book manuscript that I fully intended to eventually publish. The writing, which took me about six months to complete, certainly helped me get things off my chest and was, as others had predicted, extremely therapeutic.

I showed the manuscript to a number of people, who all encouraged me to seek a publisher. I chose, instead, to put the pages in a drawer, where they remained for over 20 years. My original reason for putting the manuscript away was that, when I originally put pen to paper, some details seemed too sensitive to share with the world.

In particular, I wanted to protect my two sons, who were very young at the time the events in this book occurred. The main part of the story is a horrific accident that had been witnessed by both boys and surely had added enough emotional pain and fear to their young lives. And although they had observed another significant portion of the story, the deterioration of my marriage to their mother, they had been, for the most part, shielded from the underlying causes of that break-up. So until they reached adulthood, a big part of me felt it was best to keep my manuscript in a drawer and thereby spare them any further emotional turmoil.

Now my sons are grown men who are well able to decide for themselves the rights and wrongs of what I acknowledge is a one-sided telling of events that had a tremendous impact on their childhoods. So, in 2004, I decided to commit myself to publishing my story. My hope is that people facing the type of intense physical and emotional challenges that I experienced when I cheated death for the third time will take courage from what they read here. Also, I hope that anyone who is facing the havoc and hopelessness that surround the breakup of a marriage will take hope from the part of my story that proves that you can find love the second time around.

Thus, man's fate often seems to hinge on one single insignificant moment in time.

–Karl May, German author

I

On May 12, 1979, a seemingly insignificant moment altered nearly every part of my life and that of my family. The day started off pretty much like any other Saturday at my family's home in Westford, MA, an outer suburb of Boston. It was the one full day of the week that I spent with my sons, Stephen, age 5, and David, age 3-1/2. Some Saturdays we played, read stories, went to McDonald's for breakfast, or did miscellaneous errands.

Today began with breakfast at home. My wife, Anne, usually cooked a full meal—home fries, bacon, poached eggs, coffee, and juice. The kids loved the togetherness, especially because their sense of security had been badly jarred in the previous year when problems between Anne and me had caused me to move out twice, once for a week and once for several months.

Although our marital issues were far from resolved, I had been back home for five months on this bright spring morning. We got an early start on the day's chores. The lawn had to be mowed, and because the carpenter was coming Monday to put in a new kitchen floor, I had a major chore to do. The carpenter had asked me, "If you have a chance, could you tear out the old kitchen carpet? This will be a big help to me."

Anne hurriedly put dirty dishes into the dishwasher. She had volunteered to cut the lawn. We had dinner plans that evening with our next-door neighbors, the Eves, so we wanted to finish our work early.

I started by moving the kitchen table and chairs into the family room. The next task was to unplug the refrigerator and wheel it into the family room. With everything out of the kitchen, it would be easy to tear up the old indoor/outdoor carpet. As I started pulling up the carpet I noticed how damp it was in sections. I swear I could smell all the juice, eggs, and cereal the kids had spilled on it over the last two years.

As I pulled up the carpet I noticed that the rubber backing was sticking to the floor. Whoever had glued the carpet to the old inlaid floor had used a ton of glue. What originally had seemed like a one-hour job now became an all-day task. I said to myself, "I can't do a half-ass job. I should get a scraper and scrape all this rubber off." A quick check of my not too plentiful tool room produced a pair of working gloves and a dull old scraper.

As I started scraping I heard the lawnmower engine shut off. I could hear Anne hollering. I kept working away. As the shouting got closer, I figured I'd better pay attention. Anne sounded very concerned. She was hollering at Stephen, saying, "You go to your room. I don't ever want to catch you playing with matches. Don't you know how dangerous this is?"

"But, Mom, it was Jason's idea." Jason was our next-door neighbors' seven-year-old.

"I don't care whose idea it was. You know that it's wrong. You could start a fire and burn the woods down or burn yourself. Stephen, you go to your room; you're going to be punished."

Anne seemed to be handling this pretty well. She always was good at relating to the children. Normally I would jump in and start hollering, but my mind was on finishing the kitchen floor. I just supported Anne's decision and told Stephen to go to his room.

David, our youngest, seemed undisturbed. We always worried about him wandering into the road at the front of the house. As I looked out the kitchen window, David was playing peacefully in his sand pile. Gosh, he was so independent; he could play and entertain himself for hours.

Anne was still fuming. She took a break and poured herself a usual Tab. Then she went back to mowing the lawn.

I decided the scraper I had wasn't doing the trick. I asked David if he would like to take a ride to the hardware store. He quickly accepted. Soon we returned with two nice new scrapers. David was trying to help with one. The rubber backing was coming off, but the glue residue was being left behind.

The day seemed to drag by. At one o'clock we all took a break for lunch. Anne came in and made tuna fish sandwiches. Stephen was allowed to come down and eat. I tried to explain how bad it was for him to play with matches.

Just the evening before fire engines visited the forest behind our neighbors' home as some kids had started four or five spot brush fires. Luckily they were put out without problems. Katie, our next-door neighbor, was quite frightened. She said, "Our house could have burned down!" She had luckily looked out her kitchen window, saw the flames and quickly called the fire department. Now Jason, her son, and Stephen are caught with matches. Boys will be boys, I thought to myself.

It was now 2:15 P.M. I heard the lawnmower engine stop. Anne came in and said, "I'm out of gasoline. Could you run down to the station and fill up the can?"

"Sure, I could use a break."

The floor was about 90 percent complete. Except for the glue residue, it didn't look bad. Surely the carpenter would be grateful.

I grabbed the old five-gallon red gas can. David volunteered to come again. We clicked off four gallons even. The gas gauge read $3.00. We put the can in the trunk because it was quite heavy. I always liked the smell of gas. I could smell it in the trunk. We lived only a mile from the station so the ride went quickly.

I went to the mower, took the cover off and quickly poured a gallon into the tank. Anne said, "Thanks a lot," and continued with her work. David returned to his sand pile.

A thought crossed my mind: I've seen Dad use gasoline in his auto shop to soak carburetors and greasy bolts; I'll bet this gasoline could strip these three large blotches of glue off the floor. That will really complete the job.

Some time previously, I had read a warning label on the gas can that said, "Use gasoline in a well ventilated area: avoid skin contact and keep away from open sparks and flames." So to assure adequate ventilation, I opened the crankout windows over the sink, made sure the sliders were open, and opened the front door and the dining room windows. Gas sure smells. I figured I would get as much ventilation as possible.

I put on the gloves I had been wearing earlier, secured an old dishrag, poured a little gas on the rag, and wiped one section of the floor. My God, the glue wiped right off! What a job! I poured a little gas in the corner, wipe, wipe, no more glue.

Stephen hollered downstairs, "Dad, can I go out and play? It smells in here." Normally, I would have been a hard ass and said, "Stay there a while; you haven't been punished enough." But instead I said, "Okay, go out and play with your brother." Stephen came down and ran outside. I continued my work.

I heard Anne holler again. Stephen wanted to come in and get a cookie. Again for some reason Anne shouted, "You stay outside and play; your Dad is busy."

Normally Stephen would persist or wouldn't listen, but this time he obeyed, maybe because he had just been punished. Who knows! To this day Anne doesn't know why she hollered at Stephen. It was another of those insignificant moments that quickly became significant.

I continued working my way in circles around the kitchen. I kept saying almost done, just one more section, right in front of the gas stove. I was on my hands and knees in front of the stove when it happened. A puff, a terrifying explosion, knocked me right on my ass. Within seconds, the entire room was engulfed in flames, the floor, the ceiling and me. I knew I had to get out of there fast.

I ran down the hallway screaming in horror. My face felt tight as the skin and flesh quickly burned away. I looked over my shoulder; I was running so fast the air was sucking the flames away from my body. I dove onto the ground, maybe by instinct or maybe because I had seen it done in the movies. I started rolling side to side. Out of the corner of my eye I spotted Anne and the two kids come running around the side of the house.

Anne was hysterical, screaming, "Somebody please help!" As she was hollering she was also stomping out the few flames that lingered on my clothing.

2

From that point on everything was a frenzy. It was like the speeding up of the Zapruder film of the Kennedy assassination in Dallas. A second explosion occurred as the gas can blew up. I never knew that one gallon of gas is equivalent to three sticks of dynamite. Every window on the first floor blew out. I saw the storm door shatter against the side of the house, then silence as a massive cloud of black smoke funneled out the front door.

I was laying on my back shouting, "Are the kids safe? Are they out of the house?"

I couldn't remember seeing them. I saw John Resnik, our neighbor from across the street, running around the side of the house. He was looking frantically for the kids. I waited to hear his answer. It seemed like hours passed before he said, "They're both okay."

Anne was crying uncontrollably. I could see neighbors trying to comfort her; they were dragging her away. Gene, another neighbor, was panic stricken. The look on his face was of shock, horror, and despair. His bottom lip quivered; he was speechless. He pivoted on one foot, a full 360 degrees, not knowing what to do.

I felt nothing, just tightness in my face. Something inside me said, "You're hurt bad; lie still."

A stranger's face appeared over me. He said, "I'm Bill. We've sent for help. The ambulance and fire trucks are on the way."

What I didn't know was that Bill, who was visiting the Resniks, was a trained ambulance and EMT technician. This was a huge break for me since he knew exactly what to do to help me. Bill quickly got the garden hose and started to water me down, face first. He said, "This will be cold, but it will help." He systematically soaked my entire body. He commanded someone to get a pair of scissors. Bill stripped me of my clothes. My polyester socks had blown up, melted, and receded, sticking to my ankles. Bill, acting like a surgeon, took a firm hold and tore them off my ankles. I could see the skin peel away. Still I felt nothing.

Bill soaked a piece of gauze with water. He said, "Relax, suck on this, it will cool your throat." I later learned he did this to prevent swelling in my throat so I wouldn't choke to death.

Bill then proceeded to tear my gloves off my hands and the little remaining clothes he cut off with the scissors. I now lay totally naked on the front lawn. One quickly forgets modesty in times of crisis. A cool clean wet sheet soon covered my body.

I could now hear the sounds of sirens as three fire trucks pulled up in a very organized manner. The fire team executed to perfection.

A stretcher was soon at my side. "Lie still, we're taking you to Lowell General," I was told. Six men, three on each side, slid me onto the stretcher. One, two, three, pickup; the stretcher teetered, then finally stabilized.

I called for Anne, "Anne, Anne, please come with me, please come," In seconds she was at my side. "Anne, I'm scared, I'm scared. I love you, I love you."

She repeated the words I wanted to hear so much. "I love you, Georgie, I love you." Her words seemed to make me feel safe and secure.

Now, all of a sudden, it was here. The pain that had been missing arrived. God, did it arrive, with white horses and chariots. "Anne, it hurts so much. It hurts so much." She leaned over me in utter awe. I knew she couldn't believe what had happened.

As the ambulance sped along, I felt every turn in the road, the railroad tracks, intersections, the rotaries. It was like riding in a car with your eyes closed, wondering at each and every bend where you were.

I said to the nurse, "I only want to go to Mass General or Peter Bent Brigham. They're the best hospitals in Boston."

"We have to go to Lowell first; then we clear a room in Boston," she said.

"Anne, it hurts so much; it hurts so much."

Her big brown eyes were filled with concern as she said, "Please try to relax. We'll be there soon."

Something inside told me I was seriously burned. The anguished, shocked, concerned look on Anne's face confirmed my suspicions. Anne had somehow regained her composure. She seemed strong. "You'll be okay, honey, please hang on."

The siren stopped, signaling our arrival at the hospital. The rear doors swung open. Anne disappeared as a team of technicians surrounded me. Soon bright ceiling lights were shining down on me, a sight that would become very familiar to me in the days ahead. No one seemed to be talking, just looking.

Soon a distinguished looking surgeon bent over me, "Mr. Pessotti, we have to do some tests first to prep you for your transfer to Boston," he said. "I know you're in a lot of pain; we'll give you some medication as soon as we complete our tests. These tests will tell us the degree and extent of your injuries. I have a chart here of the human body. What we have to do is stick pins in your body to determine whether the burns are first degree, second degree, or third degree. The more pain you experience, the better you'll be. With second degree burns, the first two layers of skin are burned off, your nerve endings are exposed, and you should feel the pin pricks. Second degree burns will heal without surgery. If you don't experience any feeling from the pin, this means the burns are third degree. That's very serious. Your top three layers of skin are missing, including nerve endings. You'll experience no feeling. Can we get started?"

I nodded my head.

"Okay, let's start with your legs and work up. Can you feel that?"

I tried hard but felt nothing.

"How about that?"

Negative again.

"And that?"

Negative again.

I started getting scared; I couldn't feel the needle at all. I knew my situation was serious.

Ah, now it happened. Pain, beautiful pain!

"Yes, yes, I can feel it, I can feel it!" Instantaneously excitement returned to my voice. "Good, good," the doctor said.

The needle pricks seemed to go much quicker now. Every time the needle made a mark, so did a technician with a magic marker. Finally, the technician had a chart of my body with three different colors, representing first, second and third degree burns. The chart was well marked. The chart showed that 85 to 90 percent of my body had been scorched. My condition was considered extremely critical.

Now at last came the long awaited pain medication, just enough to take away the curse. "Not too much. We want you to be somewhat alert. We'll let you know when we get transfer clearance from Boston," the doctor told me.

I drifted from being alert to periods of extreme drowsiness. The clock on the wall read 4:29 P.M. The hands didn't seem to move.

"Any luck yet?" I asked the nurse.

"No, we're still waiting to hear."

The clock now read 5:30 P.M.

"Any word yet?"

"Yes, Mass General has no beds available; we're trying to get you into Peter Bent Brigham."

Because I wasn't familiar with hospital procedures, it all seemed to be taking far too long. Finally, at 6:30, the nurse said, "We have a room at Peter Bent." If Peter Bent had been full, I would have faced possible transfer to an out-of-state hospital.

Again the ambulance doors swung open. I don't recall seeing Anne. Later I learned she had been sent home. There was very little she could do. The next 12 hours would prove to be critical.

I asked the ambulance driver what route he was taking to the hospital.

"We're going Route 128 to Route 9."

"That's the long way," I said. I was very familiar with Boston, so I said, "Take the Mass Pike to the Brighton exit at the Coke Plant, Storrow Drive to the Boylston Street exit and cut through the Fenway at the Museum of Fine Arts." I knew my directions would get us there sooner, but the driver said, "We have a set course; we've radioed ahead." The nurse next to me asked me to remain calm and relax.

The morphine shot had now taken hold; the pain seemed to be more bearable. I dozed and drifted into a very relaxed state. I drifted back to consciousness as the ambulance bounced over the trolley tracks in Roxbury. Finally we arrived at the hospital entrance marked Emergency.

A team of attendants quickly but methodically wheeled me out of the ambulance and headed me towards the Operating Room. I drifted between alertness and semi-consciousness, but never totally lost consciousness.

I could feel a lot of tightness and swelling in both my face and arms. The pain was again beginning to return. A surgeon quickly entered the room.

"Chart, nurse."

"Here, Doctor. Condition report: second-third degree burns, 85 percent body, type of accident–gasoline explosion. Morphine count–10 m.g., time 4:30."

"Mr. Pessotti, we're going to give you another shot to relieve some pain, okay?"

I nodded my head. "Mr. Pessotti, you have a lot of swelling in your left arm. We're going to do a procedure called an escharotomy. It's an incision to relieve pressure. You're losing circulation in your fingers because of the swelling. Try to stay conscious as much as you can; you won't feel any pain."

I nodded my approval. My left arm had swelled to triple its normal size. The surgeon carefully placed his scalpel on the center line of my wrist and with one steady motion slowly sliced from my lower wrist to my upper bicep. In one quick, spurting motion my arm burst open at the seams like a broken zipper on a pair of trousers! My head banged against the pillow. I felt no pain but the sight was incredible.

Now my arm was turned and the procedure was repeated on the underside of my arm. Again, the razor sharp scalpel split the under arm like a sharp ax splitting wood. I recall the doctor saying, "Pack the wound." I drifted into semi-consciousness.

On the outside world, trauma, shock and horror quickly spread to family, friends, business associates and relatives.

The OR doors swung open. I recall seeing my brother Tom leaning over the bed saying "Hang in there, man. We're here. You'll be okay."

Tom's face seemed contorted. I was concerned about Mom and Dad. "Tell them I'm okay, Tom."

Anne and the children were being taken care of at the Resniks in Westford. John Resnik, a pharmacist, was very comforting because of his knowledge of medicine. His strong, persuasive, caring character would quickly become a source of strength for Anne and the boys.

My older brother Zig, a nickname for Jack, was busy quizzing the resident doctor on my condition. "We've sent him to the Intensive Care Unit," the intern told Zig. "His condition is critical but stable."

"What are his chances?"

"At best fifty-fifty. There is a strong risk of infection. We're filling him with antibiotics."

"Should his wife be here?"

"There is not much anyone can do."

"Should I call her? She should be aware of his condition."

Zig decided to call Anne at the Resniks. Anne quickly came to the phone. "Anne, things aren't good. The doctor said there's a fifty-fifty chance he'll survive the night. All we can do is pray."

The stability that had arrived at the Resnik home quickly left. Anne went into a panic, crying, "He can't die, he can't die." She threw the phone against the wall. John quickly took the phone. Kay, John's wife, held Anne and tried to comfort her. John proceeded to blast Zig. "What the hell are you doing calling here, just when we had things quiet?"

"John, the doctor said Anne should be aware. There's nothing we can do but pray."

Mom was alone at home when the phone call came. Dad had gone to the Pigeon Club, where he raced homing pigeons as a hobby. He was out for the evening entering his pigeons in a weekend race.

"Mom, this is Jack, sit down, relax, I have some bad news. Georgie was in a fire; he's badly burned." Without over-alarming Mom, Jack tried to easily let her down. "It's serious, Mom. Stay there and pray. Tom and I are here at the hospital for the night. I'll keep you posted of any changes."

Panic set in. Mom was afraid to call the club and tell Dad. "I shouldn't tell him over the phone," she thought, "I'll have to wait for him to return." Dad was recuperating from a major heart attack seven months earlier.

Mom prayed and prayed. Each minute on the clock seemed like and hour. Two and a half hours later, at 10:30, Dad pulled into the yard at the lower garage. Mom looked out the window. As he always did, Dad went into the pigeon coop to make sure his birds were okay. She saw him switch the light off and walk towards the house.

"What will I say," she worried. "How can I not shock him?"

Dad entered the house. "Jean, are you still up?"

"Yes, upstairs, Paul."

Dad reached the top of the stairs and saw the worried look on Mom's face. "Paul, I have some bad news. Georgie's house caught fire this afternoon. He's in the hospital; we're not sure how bad. We can go tomorrow. We have to pray."

They stayed awake all night saying the rosary.

3

The next morning I awoke in a very unusual manner. I was awake, but I couldn't see. Panic set in. Maybe I'm blind. I called out, "Nurse, nurse, help me! It hurts. I'm scared."

I felt a hand at my side. "Mr. Pessotti, I'm Dr. O'Connor. Please relax, you're okay. You're in the Intensive Care Unit at Peter Bent Brigham. Your face is very swollen. You won't be able to see for three or four days until the swelling goes down. Your condition is very critical, but you're stable. We're monitoring you 24 hours a day. You're in the best burn unit in Boston."

"How serious am I?"

No response.

"How serious?"

"You're critical. There a one chance in five you'll survive, but you're young and strong. You're in for a big fight and challenge. We'll give you our best."

Not being able to see put extra stress on my other bodily senses. I seemed to hear every whisper. Suddenly my sense of smell seemed to be shocked with a pungent smell. A rotten odor, I can't describe. "What's that smell?" I asked myself.

Suddenly I realized it was the atrocious smell of burned human flesh. My own burned flesh!

It was now Sunday morning, which happened to be Mother's Day. I knew Mom and Dad would want to visit me; I knew my appearance would be a terrible shock to them and this caused me great worry. I could feel the swelling in my arms. They seemed as heavy as lead pipes. Both legs had swollen to twice their normal size. They had inserted a catheter tube, so I never had the urge to urinate.

Rosemarie, my daytime nurse, entered the room and introduced herself. I would grow fond of Rosemarie; her firm but caring ways would be good medicine in the weeks ahead.

"Okay, we've got to get you up to get a little circulation going," Rosemarie said. "Let's get your exercises out of the way. You'll have visitors later. We've been swarmed with calls. I'll help you around. We'll hang your IV lines to this pole, including the catheter. I'll give you your morphine shot at 8:30

after breakfast. Then we'll review your diet."

Rosemarie hit the automatic device that caused the head of the bed to rise up slowly. It was weird; I could hear all these sounds but couldn't see anything. The previous day, the thought had not crossed my mind that I could be blind or may have sustained eye damage because of the explosion, but now I began to worry about this possibility.

"All right, let's try to sit up. Hold my hand." I felt a firm grip.

"All right, pull." I pulled and felt instantaneous pain in my back. I was stuck to the green sheets on the bed. The open wounds were leaking body fluids and sticking.

Rosemarie slowly peeled the sheet off my back, inch by inch. The pain was excruciating. I could feel the skin peel off.

"Now let's dangle your legs, pivot yourself and turn around." I could feel pain in my buttocks; they were also sticking to the bed. As a matter of fact, there weren't too many areas of my body where I did not feel pain. My feet slowly touched the floor. Rosemarie said "I'll help you walk once around the room. I'll change the sheets while you're up."

Slowly, inch by inch, my feet moved forward. I knew not where I was going. "There, fine. How's that feel?"

I said nothing. All I could feel was throbbing pain. The pain seemed to make noises, because it drowned out any conversation. I knew Rosemarie was talking, but I couldn't hear her. All the nerve endings in my body where throbbing and pounding in unison. I found myself wishing for the morphine shot. I guess I walked around the room. I can't remember.

"Okay, back in bed. Good job! Now you can relax."

It felt so good to lie down. One short trip around the room had exhausted me.

"Let's review your diet," Rosemarie said. "The IV line in your arm is a source of food and fluid for your body. There are also antibiotics in the line to help prevent infection. Your body is going to require a large caloric intake. Your system will be trying to heal and regenerate skin, cells, and tissue. This requires much energy and will use up calories at a phenomenal rate. We have some high calorie frappes that you'll be drinking. Please force yourself; your body needs lots of calories.

"I'll get you your morphine and then we can start your morning bath," she added. "Let's get you cleaned up before your family arrives."

The morphine took about 20 minutes to take effect. It was a slow, relaxing high. I was amazed how it took away the curse of pain. Its effects would last about three hours and then the pain would gradually return.

"Time for your morning bath," Rosemarie said.

The word "bath" made me think of a warm relaxing tub with warm water and lots of soap bubbles; it sounded peaceful and calming. But this was a very different kind of bath, and it would prove to be one of the most painful procedures of my hospital stay.

First, the existing bandages were slowly removed. There were two wrappings. A fine mesh gauze with a white healing cream called Silvadene, directly covered the open wounds. This gauze was then wrapped over with white rolls of gauze called Curlex. Upon removal, these bandages would stick to the open wounds, causing pulling, tearing, and excruciating pain.

Second degree burns leave nerve endings exposed to the air. The interaction of air with these nerves causes great pain. Each limb was treated separately after removal of the gauze. A warm towel soaked in Betadine solution (like iodine) was wrapped around the open wound. This was supposed to kill bacteria. After removal of the towel, the open areas were then rewrapped with fresh Silvadene soaked gauze and covered with Curlex. The wrappings served as a temporary layer of skin. It was a relief to have the air blocked out by the new bandages.

This procedure was repeated on both arms, both legs, and upper body. Depending upon the nurse, this bath took anywhere from 90 minutes to three hours. Even with the morphine the pain at times was unbearable.

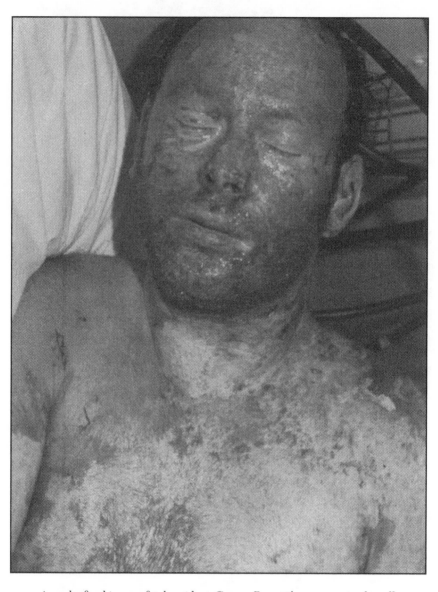

A week after his near-fatal accident, George Pessotti's eyes remained swollen shut due to swelling caused by the extensive second-degree burns on his face. Unable to see his visitors—or to look in the mirror to see for himself the extent of his burns—George listened closely to the tone of visitors' voices to gauge the devastation caused to his body by the fire.

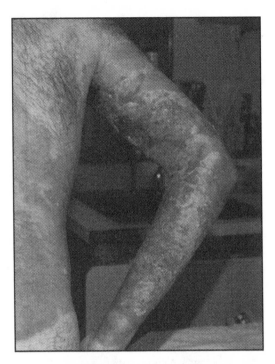

Third-degree burns covered George's legs and right arm. Unlike the second-degree burn areas, all nerve endings had been destroyed and new skin could not grow. Skin grafts taken from George's upper thighs were placed on these areas during two surgeries that occurred in his initial 70 days of hospitalization.

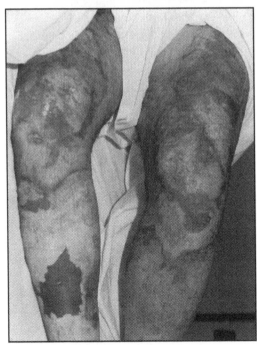

4

I couldn't wait for a familiar voice. At 11:00 A.M. the first visitors arrived. Anne came with John Resnik, our neighbor. I could hear the nurse briefing them in the hallway: "We have very strict restrictions—no bacteria allowed in the room. You have to wear the following sterile garments—hat, mask, rubber gloves, gown, and shoes. The radium light over the door will kill any germs as you enter. When you leave be sure to disrobe in the room. You can go in now."

I could hear cautious feeble footsteps coming closer. A cautious voice said, "Georgie, Georgie, how you doing?"

"Anne, Anne, is that you?"

"Yes, I'm here with John." There was silence between words. I knew their curious eyes were scanning my body. Little did I know that what they were looking at was a body that looked like a swollen hot dog that had been left too long on a barbecue grill.

John's firm voice broke the silence. "How are you feeling?"

"I'm doing okay, really I am. What a stupid thing to do, use gasoline near a stove with a pilot light. I can understand a dumb Pollock like you cleaning with gas, but I guess the dumb wop really did it." This brought a chuckle from John.

"How're the kids, Anne? How's the house?"

"The kids are fine. We've moved into the Resniks temporarily. The house is badly burned but can be rebuilt. Don't worry; we have insurance."

Anne seemed to be very strong and very much in control. In the days ahead her armor-like strength would help hold everyone up.

"Anne, could you do me a favor? I have two people meeting me at Martha's Vineyard today to look at land. Could you call them and please explain? Also cancel my appointments for the next two weeks."

"Okay, honey, don't worry about business; just work hard and get better. We love you. We're okay. Please hang in there."

"Give my love to the kids." I could feel Anne's grip on my hand tighten.

"I'll be in again tomorrow. Get some rest, okay?"

Anne sought out Dr. O'Connor to get an opinion. "George is critically ill," he told her. "He will be in the hospital for six months to a year. He's

85 percent burned. He will need surgery later on. His biggest risk now is infection. He has so many open areas that he's susceptible to many infections. The odds are not good."

Anne quickly responded, "Dr. O'Connor, you don't know George. He's no average slob off the street. He's a fierce competitor, highly motivated, and very positive minded. He won't give up too easy. You wait and see. He'll surprise you. He's a fighter."

Back at the ICU, I awaited my next visitors, Mom and Dad. The nurse repeated the message about the sterile room procedure. I could feel their eyes looking around the room. I was worried about Dad. A massive coronary less than a year ago had taken its toll. I knew Mom and Dad loved me, and that they both had been worrying and praying the entire evening before. As I learned later they practiced saying, "We have to be strong when we see George. We can't break down. It won't be good for him. We can't cry; we have to be strong."

Their emotions would be severely tested in the next five minutes. Later, Mom recalled, "I'll never forget your face, swollen, eyes shut, eyebrows, eyelashes and hair burned and singed off."

I felt their presence at my side, Mom on the right side, Dad on the left. They didn't know where to touch me. They couldn't kiss me because of the masks they had to wear. They gently held my hands. I could hear them struggling to hold back the tears.

I broke the silence. "Happy Mother's Day, Mom! What a hell of a present this is for you, Mom. I'm so sorry to put you through this."

"Oh, Georgie, it's okay. We love you. You're going to be okay. God will spare you. I know you'll be okay."

Dad still said nothing, but I felt his presence. "We'll be in again soon. Don't forget your prayers; you need God's help," Mom said.

"Okay, Mom and Dad, please don't worry. I'll be fine."

Dad patted me on the head, turned and walked away. I could hear his nose sniffling as he choked back tears.

Only four visitors and I was exhausted! The balance of the day was taken up with blood tests, x-rays, EKGs, IVs and, oh yes, shots.

5

Monday morning brought joy and a new experience. My God, I can see, I can see, but, oh, do I really want to see? Already everything seemed like a dream. Did this really happen? Is this me lying here in this bed? No, it can't be, I'm usually at work by now hustling my tail trying to make a buck. No matter how hard I tried, the reality wouldn't go away.

Rosemarie entered at 7:00 A.M., her usual time. She said, "Today you're going to the tank." "The tank? What's that?"

"Oh, it's a big tub they'll soak you in to help the healing."

It sounded so benign and rather peaceful; little did I know!

After breakfast Rosemarie entered with the by now familiar needle.

"Time for your morphine; you'll need it for the tank," she said.

Usually within 15 minutes I could feel the effect, a very relaxing drug. It sure took the edge off the pain.

Rosemarie said, "Relax. Escort will be here at 8:15 to take you to the tank."

At exactly 8:15 a stretcher was pulled up outside my room. The stretcher was covered with plastic. Rosemarie wheeled the stretcher into the room and asked the person from the Escort Department to wait outside.

"Okay, George, tank time, let's go."

The stretcher was no more than 12 feet away from the bed, but it seemed like a mile. As I tried to sit up I could feel my back sticking to the sheet. The smell of burned flesh was still horrendous. Inch but inch my arms helped push my butt to the edge of the bed. I feel dizzy as I sat up. It was ten full minutes before my lead pipe legs touched the floor. Rosemarie was there to give me balance.

Step by step this battered body scuffled across the floor. It felt so great when my hands clasped the side of the stretcher bed. Now all I had to do was get on it. No problem, I'll just step up on this little stool, pivot and lay down. Not so quick, my legs felt so heavy. It took at least five tries of each leg to lift them eight inches onto the stool, slowly pivot, nice and easy. I could feel the cold stainless steel railing against the back of my legs. I sat down and fell back in sheer exhaustion. So much energy had been expended.

Rosemarie stayed beside me all the way to the tank, which was in the basement. People stared as I was wheeled past lockers, the cafeteria, and labs. All the pipes in the ceiling had colors. The water mains were red, gas pipes green, sprinklers were red, drain pipes were black. Each sprinkler station had a number; all the walls were painted different colors. This view would become all too familiar to me in the weeks ahead.

We finally arrived. "George, this is Cheryl; she's in charge here, I'm going back to your room to change your bed and prepare your bandages. I'll see you soon." With that, Rosemarie pivoted and left.

I immediately felt panicky. In just two days I had become dependent on Rosemarie. This was my first venture outside my new home in the ICU. Who are these new people? What are they going to do to me?

Cheryl spoke up, "Relax, we're going to give you a bath, remove some dead skin, maybe exercise a little. We'll be done in 30 minutes."

That didn't sound bad. Cheryl proceeded to attach a hoist to the front of my stretcher and one to the back. I gripped the sides. A push button and a motor lifted the stretcher off of the bed. I was now suspended in mid-air. The stretcher was positioned over this large mushroom shaped tank. Slowly the stretcher was lowered into the warm water. Immediately I felt pain, a burning tingling sensation all over my body. I wanted to cry out, my heart beat quickened, and my eyes filled up. I couldn't believe the pain.•

"Are you okay?" Cheryl asked.

A quick side-to-side motion of my head gave her a negative reply.

"Hang tough. They didn't give you enough morphine. Everyone's pain and resistance level is different. Tomorrow we'll give you more morphine."

I tried to relax, but couldn't. Two therapists worked with scissors cutting off my bandages while I was in the water. Cheryl quickly worked on the open areas with a set of tweezers, removing dead skin. This is called debriding, something I would become very familiar with in the weeks ahead.

"The tingling sensation is the chlorine in the water; it helps kill germs and bacteria," Cheryl explained. "The tingling will go away within a week, as new skin starts to grow."

---

*I later learned that tanking was so painful that it was considered barbaric by many caregivers and had been banned in some burn centers. And in those places where the practice is still used, hydrotherapy, as it is now called, is made tolerable by the much more aggressive approach to pain management that is used today. The other problem with tanking was that as Barbara Ravage writes in her 2004 book, *Burn Unit* (New York: Da Capo Press), it was the equivalent of "dunking [a patient] in a bacterial soup" (162), in which bacteria could easily move from one part of the body to another. It was probably good that I knew none of this when I went into the tank!

A week? My God, I thought, I can't wait 15 minutes to get out of this tank. I was delirious with pain. I can't remember doing any exercises, but the therapists were working on my arms and legs.

"Okay, all done for today, out you come." The pulley raised the stretcher out of the water. I immediately felt chills; my entire body was shaking, as cold air hit all these exposed nerve endings.

As my body quivered a bacteriologist dabbed several areas with cotton Q-tips, slid them in sealed test tubes and sent them to the lab for testing. Microscopic analysis would tell the doctor the germ and bacteria levels in the burned area.

Cheryl quickly lowered me onto the stretcher and immediately covered me with five blankets. "You've been through the hardest day at the tank," she said. "Every day will get better. We'll give you more morphine tomorrow to make you more comfortable."

Cheryl called Escort to bring me back to my room. It sure was good to see Rosemarie. My room was tidy, bed changed, and everything in order.

A hospital photographer was anxiously waiting. He asked if it was okay to take pictures. I asked why! He explained that many interns studied photos of burn patients as part of their training. He also said many people used these slides for any potential lawsuits that might arise as a result of their burns.

I replied affirmatively. Within five minutes he snapped at least 20 pictures of almost every part of my body. I don't know how Cheryl Tiegs puts up with all those flashbulbs. I felt like a candidate for *Playgirl*, but I was pretty sure I would not make the centerfold in my present condition.

I never realized how important my skin was until I didn't have any. Exposed nerve endings monitor hot and cold. After returning from the tank I lay totally naked, exposed to the cool air, my body shook with chills and goose bumps. It was extremely painful.

Over my bed was an oval shaped plastic heat shield that could be lowered. This plastic bubble really helped take the chills away.

Rosemarie and I soon developed a routine. I watched TV game shows while she worked expeditiously to re-bandage my open wounds. My thanks to "Card Sharks," "The Price is Right," and "High Rollers"; you helped keep my mind on your shows and not my body. We hurried to finish the dressings by 11:30. Anne usually arrived by noontime. I always looked a little better with clean dressings.

On Tuesday Rosemarie said, "I'm going to try to give you a shave." I have a heavy beard and three days of growth was beginning to show. My face was full of scabs with hair growing through the scabs. My face was bumpy with craters like the moon. Rosemarie did the best she could with the straight edge razor. Each stroke would quickly fill the razor with dead skin and hair. What a procedure. Crude but somewhat effective.

Anne arrived on schedule. I was curious as to how the family was doing. The Resniks had responded with tremendous love and support. Everyone in the household co-operated. In other news from the outside world, my business partner, Dick Valentine, had hired a private adjuster to help settle the insurance claim. A mobile home would be dropped in the backyard so Anne and the boys could have a place of their own.

The mail woman arrived that afternoon. She asked, "Are you George Pessotti?"

"Yes."

"I have a lot of cards for you."

Sixty-five to be exact! I couldn't believe it. Friends, relatives, business associates and family. An incredible outpouring of love, sympathy and prayers, including 15 Mass cards. I swear the whole state was praying for me!

Some messages I'll never forget. A letter from someone I didn't even know moved me tremendously. It read:

> Dear George:
> My name is Byron MacDonald. I live in your hometown of Westford. A neighbor told me about your accident. I'm 77 years old. I was a burn patient at Peter Bent Brigham Hospital four years ago. I know how much pain and suffering you are experiencing. I have also conquered cancer and chemotherapy, which is extremely painful. When I heard that you were burned over 85 percent of your body, I knew you were experiencing twice the pain I endured. Let me say, be strong, don't lose faith in God and believe me in time the pain will go away. My prayers are with you.
> Sincerely,
> Byron MacDonald

When I read that letter, I couldn't hold back the tears. How touching! How thoughtful! This man doesn't even know me. All of these people served as an inspiration to me. I can't let them down. I won't die. They all love me. I won't disappoint them.

6

Enter Intern Dr. Beede. "Mr. Pessotti, you're not getting enough calories; we're going to put a tube up your nose and into your stomach to force feed you."

How detestable! I pleaded, "Please give me a chance. I can drink more frappes. Those tubes repulse me. They make me hyperventilate and regurgitate."

"I'm sorry, but your life is at stake. We can't take a chance. Swallow this water; it will help the tube go down."

Inch by inch a two-foot plastic tube disappeared up my nostril. I kept gagging and choking. It felt terrible. As in the past, my system seemed to reject this foreign device. I kept gagging.

"Relax, relax, you're upset. Please calm down. You'll get used to this tube."

I coughed and choked for the next seven hours. I was even spitting blood. Around 9:00 P.M. the X-ray technician came in and said, "We need an X-ray to make sure the tube is in its proper place before we start feeding you. Sometimes the tube ends up in your lungs. It would be disastrous to pump frappes into your lungs."

Twenty minutes later Dr. Beede returned with an X-ray in one hand and a puzzled look on his face. "We can't find the tube, it doesn't show on the X-ray."

It turned out that the tube had coiled in my throat. I now knew that seven hours of extreme discomfort was a result of the tube being misplaced. I was furious.

"You get that goddam tube out of my throat. No more tubes. You get that dietician in here tomorrow. I'll show you how many frappes I can drink. Now get the hell out of here." The intern went scurrying with his tail between his legs.

The next morning at 7:00 A.M. sharp, Pat, the dietician, came in. "How many calories do I need to heal at a rapid pace?" I asked. "Around 8,000 calories a day," she answered.

"How many calories in one 12-ounce frappe?"

"Roughly 250 calories."

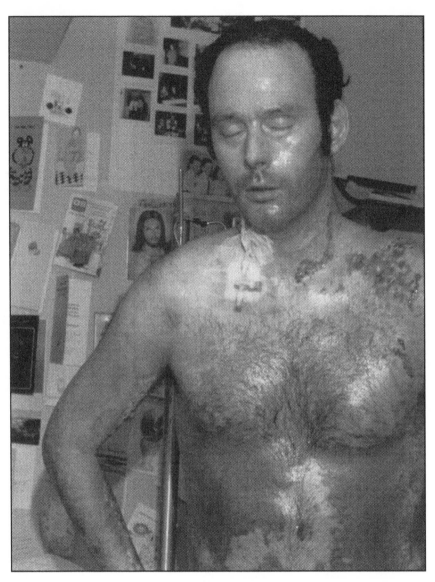

Thirty days after the fire, the burns on George's face showed much improvement, but the deep second-degree burns on his left shoulder and neck had already started to develop significant scarring. The wall behind him shows a small sample of the hundreds of cards and keepsakes sent to him by caring family members and friends during his hospitalization.

"If my math is right that's about 32 frappes a day, right?"

"That's right, but you'll have to work hard. That's about 12 quarts of fluid."

"Can you put a graph on my wall and mark my calorie count each day?"

"Sure, we can do that."

"Okay, you've got a deal."

For the next weeks, I worked my tail off. Banana frappes, vanilla, chocolate, strawberry. Work, work, work. Day one: 7,000 calories. Day two: 8,000. Day three: 9,000. On day four, I went off the chart with 10,800 calories. The hospital staff couldn't believe it. Dr. Beede couldn't believe it. Every time he walked by I'd raise my arm and show him a frappe as much to say, "I'll prove you and your tube were wrong."

My body quickly responded and accepted every calorie I could give it. I could almost picture these little Leprechauns in my stomach anxiously awaiting these calories. Okay, boys, here comes some more energy. Oh, let's grab it, run, hurry, carry this energy to all the areas that hurt.

My body used up every calorie. I didn't gain one ounce of weight. I had so much sugar in my blood that my pancreas couldn't produce enough insulin. I became diabetic. I required insulin shots every day to offset my high sugar content. My body started healing at a phenomenal rate. Nobody could believe the progress I was making. Normal scheduling for post-burn surgery is two to three months. I would be ready in four weeks.

7

A nne said the kids were anxiously waiting to see me. Dr. O'Connor thought it would be good for them to see me. We planned a Sunday visit. I was excited. I couldn't wait to see the kids. How would they react? What did I really look like? For two weeks I refused to look in the mirror. What does my face look like? Will I be disfigured?

I could hear Anne and the boys in the hallway. Their voices came closer. The nurse instructed the children on how to suit up. I anxiously waited.

Two small faces appeared. They looked like little Halloween trick or treaters with masks, oversized rubber gloves on their tiny hands, folded hats, gowns and shoes. They slowly moved forward. Anne had a hand on each shoulder. They just stared with curiosity in their little eyes. Dead silence filled the room.

Anne prompted, "Ask your Dad how's he doing."

Still silence. I wondered what was going through their minds.

Stephen broke the silence. "I love you, Dad."

David quickly followed suit and told me he loved me. Then he told the truth as only a kid can.

"Dad, you look like a monster."

Most of the five minutes was spent just staring. I wanted so much to hug them. My eyes were filled with tears of joy and sorrow, and the tears trickled down each cheek. Words couldn't express all the thoughts that went through my mind. I felt guilty. I felt the kids were being cheated. The kids had missed me greatly during the long separation Anne and I had gone through four months prior to the fire. Now, again, their dad wasn't there for bedtime stories, prayers, baths, baseball, or rides on the tire swing.

My thoughts were jogged back to reality. Anne said, "Tell Dad you'll see him next Sunday. Get some rest, George. This has been a hard day, but it is for the best that the kids see you. We're doing fine. I'll see you tomorrow."

Anne's caring attitude that day was typical of her reactions during the early stages of my recovery. The marital problems we were having prior to the fire seemed to disappear. Anne exhibited more love, caring, and compassion than I had seen the last two years of marriage. It was very comforting. One hundred percent of my time was being funneled into getting myself better. Maybe the accident would solve the problems we were having. I was sure now that Anne loved me, a feeling I had desperately missed in the past two years. Maybe this could be a rebirth of our relationship. I certainly hoped so.

Two more weeks passed by with little change in my daily routine. A fine layer of new skin started to grow over most of the second degree burn areas. Because of this, my visits to the Hubbard soak tank became more tolerable. The chlorine in the water was somewhat repelled by the new skin.

I even found myself looking forward to the tank. Cheryl, the burn technician, was most helpful. Her knowledge of burns impressed me. She kept me more informed than the doctors. As I lay in the tank, I thought how awful my body looked. Cheryl kept reassuring me that I was healing well. We could now determine that most of my third degree burns were on my left arm and both legs from the knees down. There were a few other third degree areas that would require patching.

Third degree burns require skin grafting because they will not heal on their own. A leather-like crust developed over these areas. Cheryl explained that this "escar" of crust had to be surgically removed. Fresh skin from my thighs would be transplanted to the third degree areas after the escar was removed. Science and medicine had always intrigued me, but I never thought that I would be the recipient of medical technology.

I began to take a keen interest in my body. Things happened to me that science can't explain. Somehow my white corpuscle blood count quadrupled to help fight off bacteria and infection. Some mechanism seemed to say, "Okay, this dude is really hurting; let's get together and reproduce and try to help him."

Mother Nature then kicked in by informing the involuntary muscles in my heart to pump faster so that re-oxygenated blood could speed to the burn areas at a faster more frequent pace. My normal heart beat of 50 beats per minute accelerated to 150 beats per minute, triple the normal pace. Why? God only knows. Science will never solve all the mysteries of our miraculous human body.

Yet I wasn't out of the woods. I still faced high infection risks and the threat of pneumonia. Two weeks to the day after my accident, I was treated for both of these life-threatening problems. My temperature started to rise. I was burning up with fever. My temperature seemed to stabilize at 104°. Bring on the extra antibiotics. I had more tubes in my arms. The tops of my hands looked like pincushions. There just weren't many areas to stick needles and tubes. There was talk of a by-pass shunt in my shoulder. A tube could be inserted directly into a vein, with a cap. Shots, injections, antibiotics, and blood samples could be injected and withdrawn from this shunt. I was all in favor, anything to eliminate all these needles. One quick slice from the doctor's scalpel opened my right shoulder. I could see the vein as quickly and painfully a 12-inch wire was inserted directly into it. Four quick stitches, and the shunt was in place.

As long as the fever held stable, I knew I wasn't getting any worse. As Doctor O'Connor listened to my lungs, a puzzled look was on his face. He seemed to listen on his stethoscope much longer. I could read the concern on his face.

"George, your left lung is starting to collapse. I can hear much gurgling. You must work hard, breath deeply, inhale heavily, exhale 'till your lungs are empty. Inhale, keep repeating this four times per hour. The extra exercise hopefully will prevent the tissue from further collapse."

I could feel panic set in. Was this my final leg, infection and pneumonia? No way! I won't have this. Come on, George, you can do it. The fever had me on the verge of deliriousness. My sheets were constantly soaked with blood and sweat. I constantly woke up to a soaked bed.

I kept up my breathing exercises. In-out, in-out. Thank God I'm a nonsmoker. My lungs were strong from playing tennis twice a week. The exercises paid off. Two clays later a smiling Doctor O'Connor said, "Your lungs are fine, and your fever is down to 101º."

8

Cheryl started briefing me about my upcoming surgery. "The surgeon will remove that thick escar crust from all of your third degree areas," she said. "He will simply cut it off. To cover this area they will remove unburned skin from areas called donor sites. The tops of your thighs on both legs will be the donor sites. A motorized machine like a cheese cutter will strip off skin about two inches wide by 12 inches long. This machine will mesh the skin or poke holes in it. The skin will look like a spider's web. With the holes in the skin, two inches of skin can be stretched into 14 inches to cover the burn area. The open wounds on your donor sites will be sealed with a medicated bandage called scarlet red. After seven to 10 days, this bandage will fall off."

Sounded scary but intriguing to me. Cheryl also told me that I would be on bed rest for one week, which meant I'd have to lie still. "The grafted skin is not stitched," she said. "It is just laid on. Within two days the skin starts to take roots and grow. You have a lot of areas to cover; you'll require surgery at least twice."

The week before surgery I kept busy drinking frappes and exercising. I knew my body would be weak after surgery. The cards, letters, and phone calls kept pouring in. The first three weeks only immediate family members were allowed visitation. That was about all I could handle. It was emotionally draining. I had at least got accustomed to family. I no longer had to worry about what I looked like to them; they had seen the worst of it.

One night after my evening bath and dressings, I finally built up enough courage to look at my face in the mirror. I slowly peeked into the mirror. I can't describe the feeling. I looked so different. My hair down the center of my head had been shaved. I looked like a Mohawk Indian. My eyebrows and eyelashes were burned off. My lips were very scabby and cracked. The rest of my face consisted of dark brownish red patches that were peeling and flaking. The tip of my nose was white and hard, possibly a third degree burn. The ugly color ran down the left side of my throat to my shoulder. I felt hurt, shocked, scared. Could this ugly mess possibly heal?

Give it time, I told myself. The doctors were confident of no massive facial scarring. I prayed so often hoping that God could at least spare my face.

The next afternoon Rosemarie interrupted my rest. "Someone is here by the name of Mac Mitchell," she said. "He insists on seeing you."

Excitement quickly set in. "Oh, yes, please send him up. Please send him up."

Mac was my marriage counselor. He was a middle-aged, handsome minister from the Congregational Church. Mac and I had become very close three months prior to the fire as we shared intimate conversation relative to my marital problems and two separations. Mac was very aware of the mental anguish and pain I had experienced. He was a very warm sensitive person, and I had shared feelings and experiences with him that no one will ever know of. Mac was one of the most open, down-to-earth clergy people that I had ever met. He also had experienced marital problems and divorce.

My heartbeat intensified as his caring presence entered the room. His solemn face showed so much love and concern. I could read his mind, "My God, you've been though so much mental anguish the last year, now this. What can I do to help?"

My eyes darted back and forth, following his every glance, he came closer and closer and stopped at my side. My throat tightened, dryness set in, my mouth wanted to utter a thousand words, but I couldn't find the words and my eyes filled. I was fighting not to break down. I never lost eye contact.

I meekly uttered, "Mac, it hurts so much. I love you." He gently put his hand on my forehead and made the sign of the cross, never losing eye contact. He struggled for comforting words. "Peace be with you," he said. A tear rapidly descended his cheek. He turned slowly and walked away.

I knew how crushed and hurt he was. I'll never forget his presence. Visits like these gave me strength. I had so many friends who cared for and loved me.

Anne and the children arrived again the Sunday before my first surgery. I was apprehensive and scared. I tried not to show my feelings. The kids had now adjusted to my looks. They could see progress each visit.

They sat on chairs at my side and told me about their week. "We've moved into a trailer, Dad. We have bunk beds. The carpenters are fixing the house. When are you coming home, Dad? I miss you, Dad."

God, I love those kids so much. David could find the unburned areas on my body. "Can I touch you there?" he asked, as he pointed to the areas. "Can I touch you there? There?" He leaned forward and rested his head on my pillow. "I love you, Dad."

These words were often spoken by Steve and Dave. We were always open about expressing love and feelings.

"I'll be here with you tomorrow for your surgery, George," Anne said. "I'll be here bright and early."

I had felt more secure with Anne the last three weeks. She showed me tremendous strength, coverage, love, and compassion. She was fully in charge of rebuilding the house, buying new clothes for the kids, picking carpet colors, fixtures, wallpaper and appliances. Picking through the burnt rubble and making a list of personal items lost in the fire was painful for her. But even with all this on her shoulders, she hadn't missed a day visiting me, making the 100-mile round trip every day. It was a draining experience, but she showed no signs of self-pity, only strength and compassion.

That afternoon the anesthesiologist visited me to explain how they would put me to sleep. "We'll use a mixture of gas, pentathol and morphine," he said. "You'll be out a couple of hours. You'll have to do a lot of coughing after surgery because the gases build up in your lungs. There are risks, but not high risks. Everyone reacts differently. See you tomorrow. Get as much rest as you can. No eating after midnight."

That evening Chris, my evening nurse, prepped me for surgery. She shaved all the hair off my upper thighs and lower stomach area. It was a weird feeling seeing my bald legs. They hardly looked like a model's legs, but they were smooth anyway!

I couldn't sleep that evening. In the past I tried to rely on natural phenomenon for sleep and healing. I took no pain pills or sleeping pills. This night I was uptight, nervous and restless. I asked the nurse for a sleeping pill. I waited 20 minutes, still nothing, another sleeping pill, still nothing. I kept waiting, but nothing was happening. I was hyper. Chris got permission to give me Valium. Four pills later, sleep finally arrived. It arrived with a bang, like a truck had run me over. I was out until 6:00 the next morning. I arose far from bright eyed and bushy tailed. I felt lousy, and pledged never to take those pills again.

Surgery was scheduled for 1:00. Anne arrived at 11:00 A.M. We casually chatted, no heavy conversation. I was very nervous. I would soon be helpless and at the mercy of the surgeons. Escort arrived at 12:30 to take me to the operating room.

"I'll stay with you, Georgie," Anne said. "I'll be here when you come to. I love you. Please be strong. You're doing so well; don't give up now. Be tough."

As we headed towards the OR, Anne followed the stretcher like a dog following its master. The stretcher stopped at an area that said, "No visitors beyond this point."

"Okay, Mrs. Pessotti, this is as far as you go," she was told. "You can wait in the Recovery Room."

Anne kissed me on the cheek.

"I'll be waiting. I love you," she told me.

I could see the tears in her eyes. My eyes followed her to the swinging doors until she disappeared.

A nurse quickly arrived. "We're going to give you a shot to help keep your throat dry. It should work within five minutes." My throat was as dry as a camel's butt on a hot desert day. I kept swallowing, but there was nothing to swallow.

I was wheeled into the OR. I remember the room being spotless, with big spotlights. A surgeon's assistant spoke to me, "We want you to swallow this gel; it will numb your throat and make things more comfortable for the breathing tube we have to insert. Dr. O'Connor prefers this procedure to a tracheotomy."

I opened my mouth wide and felt the spray. What a terrible taste! A slimy, smelly gel; you'd think they could make it mint flavored!

Another technician explained how they would tie me down. They brought in metal arm extensions that snapped on the side of the bed. I was instructed to hold my arms straight out, my arms were then strapped down, and my legs were spread and tied down. I looked and felt like Christ did on the cross. I was getting ready to be crucified.

In walked Dr. O'Connor and two assistants.

"How are you doing, George?" he asked.

I nodded. "I'm anxious, but ready."

"Okay, let's get started."

The anesthesiologist explained, "I'll put this mask over your face. Breath normal; you'll actually smell the gas. You'll slowly go to sleep, okay?"

I nodded. It took about 30 seconds, I remember the faces getting hazy and then it was lights out.

9

The lights didn't come back on as quickly as they went out. I drifted between consciousness and semi-consciousness, feeling very drowsy. I saw faces bending over me. Their heads looked so big! Their lips were moving, but I couldn't hear anything. The room seemed to be spinning. I was confused.

"Have I gone to surgery yet?"

A beloved face helped bring temporary consciousness. I spotted Anne as part of the crowd bending over me.

I muttered, "Is it over? Is it over?"

"Yes, it's over, Georgie. Everything went well."

"How long was I in there?"

Anne paused. "Four and a half hours, Georgie. They got a lot done. Relax, you're fine."

The semi-consciousness continued as they wheeled me back to my ICU bed. I could feel some pain in the right side of my neck. I could see the rough facial outlines of two doctors; they were inserting another bypass T-clamp for injections and blood samples. I could again feel every inch of the wire as it crept up the vein in my neck. I couldn't figure out why they didn't do this in surgery while I was out cold. I guess I came to a little early.

I soon experienced new feelings of pain. My donor sights started to throb. My thighs on both legs from knees to groin had to be stripped of any unburned skin. This skin had been grafted to my lower legs. I now felt pain in my lower abdomen. A strip of skin had been cut off my lower stomach and transplanted to my left arm.

As Rosemarie had told me, the donor sites and grafted areas were covered over with a mesh soaked red gauze. This ugly, messy bandage served as a seal to hold grafts in place and also as a seal for the donor sights. This bandage literally stuck to all areas. The red Mercurochrome color made me look like I was bleeding all over. I was afraid to move. I had explicit instructions from Dr. O'Connor to lie virtually motionless for seven days until the grafts took root and started to grow and secure themselves to my flesh. After seven days I would go to the tank and have the bandages removed. At that point we would know how good or bad surgery had gone.

We would know how many grafts would take and how many my body had rejected. The higher the percentage of success, the easier the road for the second set of grafts would be.

I couldn't believe the aching and throbbing feeling in the donor site areas. I didn't realize that just under the bandages my thighs had been stripped down to raw flesh, leaving thousands of nerve endings exposed. Every time my body got a chill, the goose bumps slowly tore their way across my thighs, rattling and antagonizing uncovered nerve endings. My entire body shook. I dreaded getting chilled.

My lungs felt very full and congested. Dr. O'Connor explained that many gases had built up and settled into my lungs during surgery. He told me I would have to do a lot of coughing to blow out gases that had lodged in the alveoli, or air sacs, in my lungs.

As expected the coughing started and kept on going. Every time I would cough, my lower stomach and upper thighs ached. The tight scarlet red bandages pulled and rubbed against nerve endings, causing excruciating pain. This problem became complicated when I started throwing up. I couldn't eat or drink a thing. If I even started to sip a frappe the regurgitation process started, and the dry heaves continued and continued. This sickness lasted two days. I thought the coughing never would stop.

The second evening I was so uncomfortable that the intern team thought I could have some blocked gases in my stomach. They decided to do a stomach pump to see if they could slow down the heaving and throwing up. I'll never forget the awful feeling of that plastic tube going down my throat. A long syringe like pump was screwed onto the end of the tube. The pump handle looked like a large spray gun used to exterminate roaches. One long, slow retreat of the pump handle set my stomach gurgling. I could see ugly green and white slime fill the chamber. Unscrew and dump, re-screw and pump. This procedure accomplished one thing. I temporarily stopped complaining because no way did I want this procedure repeated.

My week of lying perfectly still was sheer boredom. I was paranoid about moving, fearful of detaching the grafted skin. How would my legs and my arms look?

I felt growing tensions and anxieties. I prayed for the grafts to take. During quiet and lonely times I found myself talking to God, letting him know how grateful I was for his sparing me. Please give me the strength to heal and fight off this ever-intruding enemy of pain, I prayed.

Letters and cards kept pouring in. Every day, I anxiously waited for the mail delivery. The walls of my room were literally a collage of cards. I would stare at the cards, amazed at how many duplicate cards there were; four different people sent the same card.

The third morning after surgery the coughing and throwing up subsided. My God, it felt so good to sip a glass of ice water! It tasted so good. My breath smelled so bad, I swear someone had shit in my mouth. That first beautiful sip of water sent the mouth dragons running. How beautiful.

Enter Rosemarie. "We've got to give you a enema. You haven't moved your bowels in three days. It's very common when you lie around in bed with no movement. Mark, a new nurse on the floor, will assist us after breakfast."

Now most people know what an enema bag looks like. I had seen one many times as a child. When we were kids, Mom would give us an enema if we looked strange in any way. I thought of the small Cape house we were raised in. This house had the most inefficient layout of any home I have ever seen. The only bathroom was right off the dining area, like three feet away. Mom would casually lay us down on the kitchen table for our weekly enema.

"Please Mom, I feel okay, really."

"No, this will clean you out."

The big orange bottle would be filled with soap and water. I swear there was five gallons in the bottle. Enter the head of the hose, and Mom would squeeze the bottle. "Oh, Mom I can't hold anymore."

"Hold more. We are almost there. We are almost there."

Thank God the toilet was three feet away. We were the most regular kids in the neighborhood.

The only difference in a ICU enema bag is the color. The principle is the same. Rosemarie inserted the tip and filled me up good. Mark assisted by watching. Rosemarie said, "I'll be right back," and left the room. I propped myself on the bedpan. I was careful not to move too much, still being afraid that I would tear the new skin grafts. The bedpan had been greased with a cream so it wouldn't stick to my buttocks. I started flowing and couldn't stop. A funny wet feeling, the shit and water was up to the rim of the pan. I could feel the wetness. I panicked,

"Mark, this pan is full, and I still have to go."

"Well, hold on, I will go dump it."

"But I can't hold anymore!"

Rosemarie came to the rescue.

"Mark, just get another pan."

Yeah, good idea.

Mark quickly returned with a clean pan. "Okay, George, lift up."

I raised my cheeks the best I could. Mark gave a quick tug. The full pan had stuck to my ass. He pulled again and it let go, a tidal wave of shit and water splashing all over Mark and the bed.

One hour later, after clean sheets and a hearty laugh, things returned to normal.

My days had settled into a rhythm that was painful at times but very comforting and secure. I counted the days on a calendar the kids made for me. The calendar was headed June 1979, each day was a collage of family pictures, drawings and newspaper clips. Somehow a month had gone by. Some days seemed like months all by themselves, and a month in some respects seemed like a day.

I had tremendous anxiety. What would my arms and legs look like? Was the skin grafting successful? How much more surgery would I need? How about infections? So many thoughts. After one week of bed rest, I knew my muscles and body were weak from lack of exercise. In a few days I would find out how weak.

Anne shared similar anxieties. She faced the anxieties of seeing and worrying about me each day and also the pressures of rebuilding a home and setting up a temporary home in a mobile trailer. So many belongings were lost in the fire, but somehow everyone pitched in and helped set up living quarters.

Anne heard hammering one morning about 7:00. Five-year-old Stephen loved to bang nails and wood. He was busy in the garage playing with scraps of the wood left over from the reconstruction that was going on. Stephen entered the trailer with a piece of plywood eight inches wide and two feet long. He had nailed four even length blocks of wood on each corner. "Mom," he said, "Here's an end table for the lamp next to the couch."

How touching and thoughtful. Even a 5-year-old was aware of how much we had lost.

10

***

Well, the big day was about to arrive. "Tomorrow morning we will take the bandages off and take a look," Dr. O'Connor told me.

I felt excitement and fear. What if the grafts didn't take?

Anne reassured me. "I will be with you tomorrow morning," she said. "I'm coming to the tank to watch."

I felt so secure. Anne was there every day, comforting me, reassuring me, and most of all expressing her love and concern for me. So many people were rooting for me.

On Tuesday morning, June 19 (my brother Jack's birthday), Anne arrived at 8:30. I could see that concerned look in her face that I had seen so often in the past few weeks.

"Are you ready?" she asked.

"I can't wait."

Successful surgery would mean that I was getting closer to discharge. I was excited and figured I would bounce out of bed and walk to the stretcher and buzz down to the Hubbard tank. But hold on; not so quick. As I sat up, I felt immediate dizziness as blood rushed from my head to my lower extremities. I forgot I had been lying still on my back for a week.

Rosemarie slowed me down. As I dangled my feet over the side of the bed, I felt something new, my lower legs started to throb as blood rushed to the newly grafted areas. Prior to surgery I had no feeling in my lower legs. The third degree burns had burned away vital nerve endings, but now I felt circulation, I felt tingling, and I felt pain. But somehow it seemed okay.

I tried to stand up, but my legs started to wobble. They were so weak I could barely support my weight. Anne and Rosemarie quickly put my arms over their shoulders.

I felt panicky. "Please hold me. I'm so weak." I felt totally at their mercy. I tried to move ever so slightly, my legs felt like lead weights, like a freshly stricken polio patient. Inch by inch I chugged and puffed towards the stretcher. It seemed so far away. The room was spinning. I felt pain.

Somehow I got on the stretcher. My heart was pounding, and I was totally exhausted. Anne was fighting off tears as she held my hand tightly. I must have appeared so disabled to her. There was silence all the way to the tank. I tried to rest. Please, dear God, let my legs be okay. I prayed so hard.

Soon we arrived at the tank, and Cheryl greeted me with her traditional boisterous,

"Good morning! Now we can take a look."

The motorized pulley slowly lowered me into the water. The warmth felt so good. It seemed like months since my last bath or tanking. The scarlet red bandage dye quickly colored the water; it looked like I was bleeding everywhere. Cheryl slowly and methodically unwrapped my first leg.

"Call Dr. O'Connor. He wants to be here," she told an assistant.

The first layer of bandage was removed. Now the grafts awaited below the last covering. Anne and I watched with great anticipation. Dr. O'Connor arrived and was busily unwrapping the second leg. The final scarlet red bandages were removed. The doctor quickly surveyed the red skin dyed areas. There was silence; my heartbeat quickened. Anne's grip on my hand tightened. Such tension until finally Dr. O'Connor broke the silence.

"Your legs look great. Most of the grafts have taken!"

I felt joy and excitement. I couldn't hold back the tears; I was crying but making no sounds. Anne did likewise as she kissed me on the cheek. I couldn't see much, just red dye. My legs looked dark purple. They didn't look good to me, but who was I to say!

"Now let's get a look at that left arm," Dr. O'Connor said. This was the one we had been so concerned about just four weeks before. Slowly the process of unraveling was completed.

"Hold up you arm," I was told.

I could see it much better than my leg.

"Looks great," Dr. O'Connor said. "Looks great. Look at that; all the grafts took. You can't see the escharotomy scars. The grafts covered those up. Very successful I'd say."

"Really, Doc, really? They look okay, do they?" I was so relieved and so excited.

"Yes, you will need some touch up work in a few weeks, but nothing major. The hardest surgery is over."

Anne was so excited she had to run to a phone to call everyone. I just lay there on the stretcher, covered up with blankets, physically and mentally exhausted. A full day and it was only 10:00 A.M.

I couldn't wait to get back to my room to tell Rosemarie how successful the surgery was. She could tell by the expression on my face that the news was good. "I'm so happy for you," she said.

11

Ifelt a new sense of excitement. Progress, a light at the end of the tunnel. The pain levels became bearable during the daytime hours. The only morphine required was for morning tanking and evening baths.

I was now more alert and aware of the daily happenings in the ICU. There were more open-heart surgery patients than you could count. One day I noticed a pounding sound. It sounded like someone beating up a patient! I asked Rosemarie what it was. She explained that the nurse next door was pounding the back of an open-heart surgery patient. After surgery their lungs build up fluid; this pounding helps keep the fluid moving in the lungs. At times the pounding seemed quite loud.

Another severe burn victim had been wheeled in. I overheard the nurses talking about him. He was 31 years old. A pickup truck had crashed, pinning his legs under the dashboard. The engine had caught fire; he had third and fourth degree burns the entire lower body, lung damage. Sounded pretty severe. I found myself praying for this unknown person. Later he went into a coma. Infections set in, and they had to amputate both legs.

I inquired daily about this man's condition. The smell of burned flesh was overpowering. Only a few nurses on the staff volunteered to care for him. Two weeks later his heart stopped and was restarted three times. No brain activity showed on the scan, but his heart kept beating. The nurses continued his care despite his gruesome appearance. Skin grafting was even done while he was in a coma. Three days later this unknown soldier died. I felt so much sorrow for his family. I guess it was a blessing. He went in peace.

Another day there was a clamor in the hallway. I kept watching the hurried activity. I noticed a man who looking quite despondent standing in the hallway. He seemed dazed, very nervous, shifting foot to foot. I knew someone in his family was badly hurt. I had seen that worried look so often on the faces of visitors. I wished I could comfort him somehow.

I asked Rosemarie what was going on. She explained that a new patient named Phyllis Bloomsack was in the room next door. Her body had developed an allergic reaction to a pill she had taken. Three weeks ago her skin had started peeling. Originally it was thought to be a skin problem, but the peeling continued. The first and second layers of her skin had fallen off, so she was experiencing the equivalent of having second degree burns over 100 percent of her body. Although she was not physically burned, the same pain and other problems applied. Somehow a team of doctors stopped the peeling. Her condition was extremely critical.

I asked Rosemarie to send the man in the hallway in. He was Harvey Bloomsack, her husband. I briefly explained my condition to him. I assured him that his wife was in the best hospital in the country. "Don't lose hope," I said. "Keep praying. She'll be alright. I'll pray for her." He thanked me for my kindness.

The next day upon returning for the tank, a thought crossed my mind. Maybe I should switch rooms with Phyllis so she could use the heat shield that was over my bed. My room was the only room with this shield. I remembered how just four weeks earlier I would shake all over from the chills and exposed nerve endings. I asked Rosemarie to see if Phyllis wanted to switch rooms. Dr. O'Connor came to see me. I wanted to be sure that whatever disease she had was not contagious before I entered her room. He assured me that it wasn't. Dr. O'Connor thanked me for being so thoughtful. "Tomorrow morning while you're at the tank," he said, "we'll sterilize both rooms and make the switch."

I couldn't wait till the next morning. I knew Phyllis would be more comfortable in my room. On my way back from the tank I was delayed at the end of the corridor.

"Your room is not quite ready yet," I was told. "They're moving all your cards and personal items."

"No problem."

As I lay there on the stretcher I noticed another stretcher approaching. The woman on the stretcher was moaning. She was red and swollen all over, half her hair was missing and she had no eyebrows. It was Phyllis Bloomsack. I now felt even better about giving up my room. She looked so bad.

Two hours later my room was finally ready. Rosemarie was busy re-taping cards on the walls. The new surroundings were a pleasant change. I liked having four new walls to study. I started teasing Rosemarie, "Can't you get this room ready any quicker? You look like a kid playing pin-the-tail-on-the-donkey."

"Well, at least I don't look as funny as you did one day." Having said that, Rosemarie quickly clammed up.

"What do you mean you don't look as funny as I did? What are you talking about?"

Finally Rosemarie said, "About four weeks back when you were swollen to twice your normal size, it was funny. One morning you slowly walked towards the commode and your back was to me. I looked over and all I could see was your balls sticking out of the cheeks of your purple ass. They were the size of oranges, you looked like a baboon."

It struck as me funny, too. We had a good laugh.

12

Three days had passed since the unveiling of the grafts. I had been dangling my legs over the side of the bed three times a day to get the circulation going. Tonight I was to try to walk for the first time in two weeks. Chris, my 3:00–11:00 P.M. nurse, would be my crutch and assistant. Little did I know how weak I really was.

After supper Chris started to prepare the dressings. "Let's get you cleaned up, change your bed, and then we'll try to walk a little," she said.

I was feeling pretty good because Mom had brought a nice stuffed haddock dish for my supper. It sure was good to taste some good old-fashioned home cooking. Three nights a week Mom and Dad came in with a hot dish. I looked forward to these suppers. I knew Mom would always bring something good. It was their way of helping. Mom was relieved when she saw me eat a good meal. Everyone pitched in bringing goodies. My appetite seemed much better. I was consuming fewer frappes because of the hearty meals I was getting.

I also looked forward to Wednesday nights, when my brother-in-law and sister-in-law brought supper all the way from Gardner, 70 miles one way. Pen and Dave brought a big pepperoni pizza and beer one night. The entire ICU smelled like a pizza parlor. I could always count on Penny and Dave.

Chris started my evening bath. It was the first time she had done it so I instructed her on the procedure. I now found myself very adept in the bath and rebandaging procedure. I had the system down to a science.

All of the prior nurses had no hang-ups about the areas to wash. All unbandaged areas were washed, chest, upper legs, private parts, and arm pits. Chris was doing a good job, but I noticed she was blushing a little and she seemed to be definitely avoiding my private parts

"Okay, all done," she said.

"Oh no you're not; you forgot to wash my privates!"

She quickly responded, "No way! You wash them yourself."

"No, Chris, it's part of your training. You must become experienced in all areas." I could see she was really embarrassed.

"You do it," she said and threw the face cloth at me. She left the room with her face red as a beet. What a drag washing myself. At least I could fantasize about the nurses. It's probably best that Chris didn't wash this area, because after weeks of no sexual stimulation, a passing glance would have been enough to get me excited.

Chris came back into the room. "Okay, let's get some exercise. Sit up and dangle your legs. We'll wrap your legs in these ace bandages for support."

I could feel the tremendous tingling sensation in my legs as the blood quickly rushed to my lower legs. I inched myself to the edge of the bed. Slowly my legs hung until my toes touched the cold floor. Chris slid on a pair of green elastic slippers. I looked like Peter Pan.

My legs were trembling. I felt no strength at all.

"I'll support you," Chris said. "Stay close to the bed. If you feel weak fall on the bed."

My 190-pounds of dead weight was no match for all one hundred pounds of Chris. Somehow she got her shoulder under mine. I couldn't believe the pressure in my lower legs. I helped hold myself up by leaning on a long counter that ran the length of the room. I used the counter as a pair of crutches. My legs just dragged along.

"How do you feel?"

"Weak, so weak. My legs are dead; I feel like I'm crippled."

"No, you're okay. You have to get the circulation going. Your muscles have deteriorated from inactivity and surgery."

The hard, thick escar tissue that had supported my lower legs was now gone due to surgery. This thick crust was replaced by a thin layer of skin from my thighs. Quite a difference.

Somehow we circled the room twice. My legs were pounding.

"Please, Chris, get me back to bed before I collapse."

I backed up to the bed and virtually collapsed onto the mattress. My heart was pounding. Chris quickly elevated both legs by sticking two pillows under each leg. Blood and body fluid was now oozing through the ace bandages. I began to get nervous, maybe the grafts fell off. Chris assured me they hadn't. The grafted, meshed skin had holes in the skin, like the spider's web I described earlier. These holes helped drain fluid, blood, pus, and bacteria. The weight on my legs literally forced all the fluids through the holes in my skin.

I knew I had a lot of work to do to regain strength. Dr. O'Connor encouraged me to get as strong as I could because in two weeks I'd be having surgery again. Then I'd be on bed rest again for seven to 10 days with no movement.

I knew if I didn't push myself now, that walking in three to four weeks would be an incredible task. I worked three times daily, pushing myself at times to the point of exhaustion. But each day I seemed stronger and stronger.

Maybe I can leave my room and walk around the ward, I thought. I decided to try. Things looked so different standing up. For weeks I had been viewing people and surroundings from a lying down position. Everyone seemed different. Some nurses were tall, some short, and some chubby.

Chris said she would follow me around the unit. My legs inched and inched. All of the nurses were so friendly. "Look who's up! You look good, George. Keep up the good work. You'll be out sooner than you think." Everyone was rooting for me.

Computer rooms, coffee rooms, countless beds and rooms with bodies and fancy equipment. The place was an impressive operation. The sheer excitement of new surroundings thrilled me to no end. I temporarily forgot about my legs. I felt like running, walking faster. My legs wanted to do so much but couldn't.

I got halfway around the ward. I asked Chris if I could rest. We sat on a chair for a while to rest. Chris's eyes sparkled as she held my hand. "You're doing so well, I'm so proud of you. It's so good to see you out of that bed."

Chris was typical of the nurses. I couldn't believe how open and concerned most of them were. They were dedicated far beyond the scope of just being nurses. They genuinely cared about my well being.

13

Tests and more tests. Everyday there seemed to be something new. One afternoon I heard a feeble knock on my door. "Hello, I'm Dr. Woo. Can I talk to you?" Hearing his name, my first hope was that he was bringing me a Pu Pu Platter.

"We're conducting some research on badly burned patients," he began. "Let me explain. Many burn patients develop a chemical in their bloodstream that somehow retards or slows down the healing process. If the chemical is present you'll heal slower, if the chemical is not present chances are you'll heal at a faster pace. This is an experimental procedure; we're hoping to identify and isolate this chemical. If we're successful, there's more hope for faster healing for future burn survivors."

I asked if the procedure was risky.

"Not at all," Dr. Woo replied.

"What will you do?"

"I'll scratch a spot on your shoulder and add a solution. If your skin scabs up in one day, it means the chemical is present. If a scab doesn't occur, you don't have the chemical present in your blood."

I figured what the hell; it would be my contribution to research. Plus I was curious to see if I'd be a slow or fast healer. Dr. Woo drew two small blue circles with a compass on my shoulder. He pricked the surface of the skin with a pin and put a round bandage over the two scratches. He said, "I'll be back tomorrow."

I couldn't wait for his return. He came back around 2:00 P.M. the next day.

"Ah, hello, back again, let's check your shoulder."

Off came the bandage. "Ah, looks good, no scab, no chemical in your blood, you're a good healer." The procedure was repeated two weeks later and again the results were negative.

Since the first series of skin grafts there were some changes in visitation procedures. I was no longer on precautions, which meant my visitors didn't have to dress up with sterile hats, masks, gowns and gloves. It was nice to see my visitors' faces. It was also an encouragement for me to know that each day that went by the chances of serious infection were reduced. Many areas were grafted, plus second degree areas had started to heal. A new thin layer of skin was forming over the open areas, systemically sealing up the openings against deadly microorganisms.

I was anxious for Anne to come. Rosemarie informed me it would now be okay for Anne to give me a kiss. I was all excited, but I knew my lips, which had suffered second degree burns, weren't in good shape. They seemed like they would never stop peeling, cracking, and flaking. I must have used a caulking gun full of Vaseline on my lips.

After we returned from the tank Rosemarie said, "Okay, let's get you cleaned up for Anne. If you're going to give her a kiss, we have to spiff you up." Rosemarie lathered my head up the same old way, with a blue plastic tub propped under my neck. My hair seemed to be growing, getting especially long in the back, and the center strip up of the middle of my head was also starting to grow. It felt so good when Rosemarie massaged my scalp. I would sweat so much when sleeping, I felt like a new man when my hair was clean.

The next procedure was my every-other-day shave. I was a good candidate for the "Gotcha" straight-edge razor commercial. Rosemarie's hand and the razor slowly dragged over my scabby face. She rinsed the razor, an ugly mixture of hair stubs and skin falling into the water in a small pail. It was a tough procedure. Rosemarie's patience impressed me. Day after day she repeated these thankless procedures.

Boy, I was ready for Anne, hair washed, clean-shaven, and newly bandaged. It was nice to feel somewhat clean.

Anne arrived on time as usual. Around 11:00 A.M. Rosemarie was briefing her in the hallway of the fact that no more sterile garments were needed. Anne rushed into the room. It was so nice to see her long brown hair, free at last of the silly-looking sterile hat, and her face, with its bubbling brown eyes and big smile. My beautiful Ali McGraw look-alike wife could fully be seen after five weeks of being hidden behind sterile garments, and I was so glad to see her!

Anne leaned over the bed and gently kissed me on the lips.

"I love you, Georgie."

We embraced cheek to cheek for a moment. I slowly raised both arms and put them around her. I squeezed her as hard as I could. God, it felt so good to hold her. Tears rolled down each of our faces. I wanted to say so much but couldn't find the words. The tears said it all.

Being off precautions meant I could now see friends who had been refused visitation rights before. Dick and Donna Mills, close friends for 10 years, called and said they'd love to see me. Being a nurse, Donna was quite concerned about my condition and progress. Dick, a former college roommate and a budding attorney, was also anxious to see me. Anytime we got together we had plenty of laughs. We'd reminisce about college days, including our cooperative Northeastern University work assignments at Ford Motor Company in New Jersey. Our stories were never dull.

Dick and Donna arrived about 7:30 P.M. after a long drive down from Concord, New Hampshire. I had just finished eating supper, and my sister Elaine was at my bedside when they entered the room. I again saw the concerned look that I had seen on so many other visitors' faces. My eyes filled up. I was so excited to see them.

"Come on in! Come on in!," I said.

I received a big hug and a kiss from Donna and a firm handshake from Dick.

"How are you doing, Georgie?" Donna asked.

Then came that other question that I had heard so many times and dreaded.

"How did it happen, Georgie?"

I felt so guilty at times in explaining my accident. I'll always feel that way because I can't help but feel stupid about my actions that fateful day. I had already told my story so many times that I had considered tape-recording my response to the question.

Donna seemed to be asking all of the medical questions. Dick stayed distant; he just looked me over. I knew what he saw was upsetting him. The room was very hot that June night, and Dick, in a feeble voice, said, "I think I'll get some fresh air."

He took two steps and started to collapse. Donna noticed Dick fainting. He was about to fall on top of me. Donna reached out in an attempt to support Dick or push him away from the bed. His dead weight shifted to the right, his right temple slammed against the counter top, and Dick buckled to the concrete floor.

Panic immediately set in. Donna started hollering, "Get a nurse. Get some oxygen.

Dick, come to! Dick, come to!"

His eyeballs were rolling backward, and he was making a gurgling sound. Donna tried to open his mouth to see if he was swallowing his tongue. Three nurses quickly entered the room.

I was so shook up my heart started pounding. I didn't know whether Dick had fainted or had a heart attack. I started crying. Maybe Dick shouldn't have seen me. I knew it upset him. I could see blood trickling down the side of his face. He sure hit his head hard.

Finally he started groaning and coming to. Donna kept saying, "Dick, are you okay? Dick, are you okay?" At last his eyes opened. He was as pale as a sheet.

"Dick, are you okay?" I asked in a concerned voice.

"Yes, I'm fine."

Dick was upset because he had upset me so much. He was somewhat embarrassed. He started to rationalize what happened. No lunch, no supper, the long drive, a hot room. I'm sure they all played a part. The nurses insisted that Dick be taken to Emergency for X-rays.

In minutes a wheelchair arrived and Dick was off and running. My heart was still pounding. I was so scared he had been seriously hurt. An hour and one half later, Dick arrived back with a Band-Aid on the side of his head. He had much more color in his face.

We now joked and laughed about it. Dick said, "Jesus, Pessotti, I come here to visit you and end up in the Emergency Ward. What the hell goes on here?"

What seemed so serious two hours ago now seemed quite funny. To this day we joke about it. But I'll never forget it.

14

Day after day friends, relatives, acquaintances and business associates trickled in. My real estate partner, Dick Valentine, was a frequent visitor. He assured me that everything was going well. He was enjoying learning of my day-to-day business activities. He said it made him realize how much work I actually did and also gave him a better understanding of the real estate business.

Dick seemed genuinely concerned about my well being. This was pleasing because Dick is a very successful, competitive, and aggressive businessman. With him, it's business all the way, all the time. Many people had commented to me that, "You can't get close to Dick personally; it's hard to know anything about his private life," but with business and making money it's another matter. Financially, everyone knew where they stood with Dick, but they couldn't get close to him personally.

One day I received a letter from Dick that touched my heart and brought me closer to him personally. It was a pleasant, caring, compassionate, and warm letter that brought me to tears.

> Dear George:
> It's 11:30 P.M. and I can't sleep. I've been thinking of you all night. I know how much pain you've gone through. I've come to realize how much you mean to me as a person. You're greatly missed around the office. I've come to realize that you mean a lot to me as a friend. I miss you and love you a lot. I'm proud of the courage you've shown me. I can't wait for you to return.
> I guess I'll leave my office now and try to sleep. Just wanted to let you know I think of you all the time.
> Fondly,
> Dick

Coming from Dick, this letter boosted my confidence. I couldn't wait to see him and thank him. I got my chance a day later. I couldn't find the words. It was a new experience to feel close to Dick and try and share with him personally.

"Thanks for the letter, Dick," I said. "It meant so much to me." He just shrugged his shoulders and said, "I meant what I said." Short but sweet, end of conversation.

Now that time had started to heal my open wounds, I started to notice new awareness, new senses and perception. Visitors would pass my room, not knowing that I had been transferred. They'd look in the old room and I was gone. From my new room across the hall, I could see the immediate panic and shock on their face. I knew what they were thinking: "Where's Georgie? He's not in his room? Is he dead?"

Then my voice would echo, "I'm over here," and I could see their relief immediately.

The bandages on my arms and my general weakness made me clumsy. I became extremely cautious with hot coffee and liquids. One morning the nurse came in to tidy up my room. I had finished my breakfast and had just started sipping a cup of hot black coffee. It was sitting majestically on my bedside table. The nurse was adjusting the extension on my TV; a stuffed animal (a cheetah monkey) was resting on top of the television. Somehow I noticed that the monkey was directly over my coffee cup, and I knew something was coming. As the nurse turned, she bumped the TV. I watched the monkey slowly tumble down.

I reacted instantly. The monkey crashed into the hot cup of coffee, spilling it all over the bed. Luckily I had moved fast enough to avoid any more burns.

Panic set in on the nurse's face.

"Are you okay? Did you get burned? I'm sorry! How stupid of me!"

"Relax, I'm okay. It was an accident. Let's keep it a secret; no one needs to know." The nurse felt stupid, but so relieved.

The shift nurse, Norma, came in and prepped me again. "We will be moving you soon, George. We could need your bed any day." She tried to warn me of a mental letdown. "You will be going from Intensive Care to a regular ward. You won't have a private nurse; one nurse covers five patients. Many times you'll have to fend for yourself. I just want to prepare you."

Somehow it didn't sink it. My only request was to have a private room.

The transfer came quicker than I thought. The next morning Rosemarie came in with a gloomy look on her face. I knew before she spoke that I was leaving. I couldn't understand her tears, but as many nurses do, she became very close to patients. When the patient leaves, it's like losing a friend, someone you have spent eight hours a day with for 50 days.

I also felt sadness. Suddenly what Norma had tried to caution me on hit home. A good-bye cake with a candle came from the nurses along with cards and good wishes, and then my belongings were quickly put into packaging boxes. Within an hour I was resting on a stretcher in a hallway, not outside a private room, but a ward.

"But where's my private room I requested?"

The new nurse, who didn't know me, coldly responded, "There are none available. You will have to stay here until one becomes available."

Panicked, I was wheeled into a large open room. Small draw curtains separated 24 stalls in a semi-circle. My large private room was now a stall, with only two feet on each side of my bed, no television, no wall space to hang mementos and cards, no telephone.

My God, it hit me so hard, I wanted to cry. I held back tears. I pushed the call button; 20 minutes later a nurse came. I asked to use a phone.

"There's one down the hallway," she said.

I had to reach Anne. I had to ask for help. I was depressed, saddened, and choking back tears. How will anyone find me, I wondered. I've got to get to that phone.

It was now 6:00 P.M. I wrapped my swollen legs with ace bandages, dangled my feet over the side of the bed and started a slow procession to find the telephone.

"I have a collect call from George. Will you accept the charges?"

"Yes!" came Anne's voice across the wire. I was so glad to hear her familiar voice.

"Anne, you have to help me!"

"What's the matter?"

"They transferred me today. I am in an open ward, 24 bodies, very noisy, lots of groans. An old man screamed all afternoon. It's like a Red Cross Station in a war-torn town. Help me. I have to get out of here. They promised me a private room. Please help, Anne."

I fought back the tears. In all my hospitalization I hadn't asked Anne for much. She was having her problems coping and keeping our family together.

"I'll do the best I can, George. I'll be there in the morning. I'll get you out of there. Please try to relax. I'll see you in the morning."

Anne proceeded to call all sorts of people, including my business partner, the hospital administrator, Dr. O'Connor, Social Services, and the Psych Department. "You have to get him out of that ward," she told them all. "He's going crazy."

I didn't sleep all night. Moans, groans, screams and other sounds of people in pain filled the air. Only a sheet separated the 24 suffering bodies in that ward. I was now only a number in Stall 7.

The morning nurse came in and said, "Boy, your wife raised hell here last night. We're moving you this morning to a semi-private room, and then to a private room."

I felt so relieved. I couldn't wait to leave that jungle.

When Anne arrived, I couldn't wait to thank her. With her assertive manner, she had by-passed hospital red tape and got the transfer. I shared with her how upset I was. By day's end I was resting in a private room in "A" Main, ground floor. Happily, this would be my final room for recovery.

15

Within days of my transfer into the new room, Dr. O'Connor said, "You could be home in a month if your second operation is a success." The six-month hospitalization estimates I'd initially heard had been reduced to 70 days, possibly thanks to all those frappes I had downed!

This news gave me new hope, new inspiration, new inner desires to work hard physically and mentally to get ready for surgery. Slowly my lead-like legs trudged up and down the hallway. The scarred areas turned so purple, they oozed so much fluid, so much swelling, and pain, but I saw a light, a goal only four weeks away. New thoughts, new hopes, new dreams, and also, unknown to me, larger obstacles to overcome. Another struggle and crisis would soon develop.

For seven days prior to the second surgery I walked, stalked, exercised, and did leg lifts and 40 sit-ups in bed each day. The physical therapist was astonished; she couldn't believe the unending day-to-day struggle I put up to be strong again and to prepare for the surgeon's blade.

From my ground-floor window I was able to observe day-to-day happenings that people take for granted. From my bed at 6:40 A.M. I saw the early comers to work, well-groomed, carrying newspapers, walking slowly and steadily through the courtyard. The second wave crossed at 6:50, walking brisker, constantly checking their watches to see if they were late. The third wave ran, dropping papers or lunch bags, struggling hurriedly to beat the clock.

As I strolled to the park bench in the courtyard I realized how good clean fresh air smelled! I hadn't sniffed it in 50 days. How beautiful the trees seemed; how peacefully the clouds moved through the sky. Some clouds looked like imaginary objects. The American flag flapped flawlessly in the air, its aluminum chain rattling against the pole. As a keyed-up businessman, had I missed or not noticed nature's true beauty, its solitude, its wonders?

Some rustling in dry branches nearby startled me. I noticed a small sparrow eagerly trying to build a nest. He was so determined; he reminded me of myself. He was trying to remove a dead leaf from a branch. My God, he struggled. He pulled. He twisted the leaf until it finally broke loose. He survived. He met his goal and flew off to continue building his nest. How had I missed these things? Life could be so beautiful.

I found myself daydreaming. What's my purpose in life? Why am I alive? What will I do when I go home? Will my troubled marriage survive? Will my business survive my absence? Will people accept me and my scars? So many thoughts filled my mind.

I thought of other times I had come close to death and survived. Why had I survived? Did someone above have some plans for me, a reason to live? I thought about the time when I was 19 and was almost electrocuted. A carpenter who was rebuilding our home had driven a nail through an electrical wire. I had noticed that occasionally I would get a shock when I touched a towel rack. I ignored it but one day I stepped out of the shower and filled the wash basin with warm water to soak my "carpenter-ridden" blistered hands. As my hands soaked in the water my arm accidentally brushed the metal on the cabinet door. Bang, an excruciating shock knocked me back against the wall. My head banged the wall, and I slumped to the floor, both nostrils bleeding. It felt like someone had hit me in the face with a shovel. Later, the doctor said that if I had been standing in the tub water and touched the metal cabinet I surely would have been electrocuted.

I had also faced death in a terrible car accident. I was driving home drunk after a high school football reunion party. Anne had laid her head on my lap, sleeping peacefully. The pouring rain thundered down upon the windshield. I could barely see three feet ahead. I slowed to 40 mph. From Lancaster, the scene of the reunion, to Lynn, where we were living, was 50 miles. If I had known that the room at my mother-in-law's house, one mile from the reunion, was to be unavailable that evening, I would not have foolishly had too much to drink.

The warm heat from the heater quickly mellowed and tired me. I felt myself drifting. When I opened my eyes all I could see was guardrails. I had to make a quick decision: hit them or avoid them. I quickly swerved to avoid them and almost succeeded. My right front tire hit the anchor post of the guardrail. It catapulted the car down an embankment. The car flipped and rolled three times before coming to a stop on its roof.

Silence met the cool December night. Mud and water covered our bodies. Anne woke up hysterical. She shook me, "Are you alive? Are you alive?" She was having a flash back of another horrible nighttime accident when she had been driving and her passenger—a man she loved—was killed instantly.

I quickly said, "I'm okay; my shoulder aches." The engine died, but the headlights shown straight ahead. A pungent odor hit me; it was gasoline leaking from the carburetor.

"Anne, we have to get out of here."

I felt around for glass. Luckily, the front and back windshields had popped. I dragged myself and my separated shoulder out the rear window. I reached in and pulled Anne to safety. An ambulance soon sped us to the hospital. Neither of us had a serious injury. The car was a total loss. Inches separated my path between a big oak tree and the guard post anchor.

Now here I was in my hospital bed, a three-time survivor, awaiting my return to society. Spared again, but not quite sure for what reason.

16

My exercising and mental concern for my next surgery paid dividends. I bounced back much quicker. I experienced less sickness from the anesthesia, but, oh yes, that excruciating, throbbing pain that once had pushed me to the brink of collapse was back again. My thighs were again the victims of the surgeon's scalpel. Only two weeks prior these appendages were circularly stripped of all available skin. Miraculously the human body re-grows skin within two to three weeks. This new skin was again stripped to complete my grafting.

Some leftover skin was deep-frozen for possible later touch-up grafting. I learned that one never grows conditioned or accustomed to pain. Needle prinks still hurt, IV lines hurt, and those ever so tender donor sites again battered my body with tongue tingling, excruciating, throbbing pain. Why can't I get used to it?

Again the doctor's orders were bed rest for seven days until the new grafts took hold. At least my prior surgery had taught me valuable routines that I now was familiar with. Thank God I learned well. Many nurses in the new ward knew very little about burn care. I had to educate them, teach them how to wrap, how to give Silvadene gauze treatment, how to develop a system to minimize my pain.

The morning after the second surgery a new nurse entered by room. She seemed cocky and bold.

"Are you ready to get up for your morning walk?" she asked.

"Are you kidding? They just grafted me yesterday! If I walk, these grafts will fall off!" Five hours of surgery and relentless pain would have been wasted.

She insisted, "Come on, doctor's orders."

"What doctor wrote that order?"

"Dr. Lahey, the intern."

"He doesn't know what the hell he's doing. I only take my orders from Dr. O'Connor."

She remained adamant, wanting to know how could I question her authority. She resented my knowing so much.

"Okay," she snapped. "Have it your way. Feel sorry for yourself. Stay in bed, see if I care."

I was hurt and angry. I said "Okay, you little bitch, you call Dr. O'Connor right now and tell him to get down here. We'll find out who's right."

Dr. O'Connor soon arrived, and the shit hit the fan! All I could think was thank God I had stood my ground and refused to get up like I'm sure many patients would have when faced with such browbeating.

I learned to question some hospital policy and routines, only for my benefit. I was becoming assertive. For the first time in my life, I put myself first. One hundred percent of my energies were directed to me and getting better.

On the evening prior to surgery I had questioned the same intern who later gave the nurse the bum advice about getting me out of bed. "It's 1:30 in the morning; my surgery is not until 4:00 P.M. tomorrow," I said. "Why the hell do you need X-rays now? Isn't it more important that I rest tonight? You can get X-rays tomorrow. I'm not waiting all night in a cold X-ray room for a technician."

The doctor apologized and said, "Gee, I guess I wasn't thinking."

I saw that many interns and doctors are like robots; they execute the science accurately, but in the area of human relations, they fail miserably. They're always in a hurry. Rushing to the next appointment or surgery, fluffing off questions, or walking away in the middle of a conversation. They never had enough time to stand still and humanely relate to the patient.

Many times hospital routines and OR schedules change because of emergencies. My second scheduled surgery was bumped one day when a paraplegic cab driver in Roxbury was brought in after being robbed and blasted with a shotgun.

Unfortunately, no one bothered to tell me about this one-day delay. I lay in my bed all day and night wondering, hoping, praying, and mentally preparing for surgery. They should have told me. This would have saved an entire day of anguish. They told me at 5:00 P.M. that I would have to wait another day, which meant another night of no food, restless sleep, and mental preparedness. Take heed, medical world; this is just one of many small errors that add to the distress of hospital patients.

This time, the seven days of bed rest sped by. The unveiling of the new grafted areas, left arm, right arm, and both lower legs proved very successful. Dr. O'Connor said the magical words, "Rest up for two weeks and then you can go home."

"Really? You're serious? I mean, no kidding?"

"I'm serious!"

My God, I've made it! All of a sudden I was flooded with new fears, new anxieties, new worries. I couldn't wait to tell Anne. She seemed floored and excited. But I read fear in her voice. My God, she wondered, he's coming home. What will I do now?

The kids were ecstatic. Each day they clicked one off.

"Only 14 days, Dad."

"Only 13 days, Dad."

"Are you coming home forever?" Stephen asked.

I quickly said, "Yes!"

I didn't realize that these words would later cause misunderstanding and new hurt for my children.

17

For 70 days Anne had shown me only love, strength and support. But now she was panicking. We had faced very serious problems in our marriage before the fire. I had worried that Anne had inherited the alcoholism exhibited by her parents. I also suspected she had been unfaithful to me, a suspicion that had been confirmed when we were in marriage counseling with Mac Mitchell. Anne's fears centered on the fact that she wasn't sure she loved me enough to stay married. On the other hand, with almost no work experience at age 29, she also feared that if we divorced, she would lose the comfortable lifestyle she now enjoyed thanks to my success in selling real estate.

None of these problems had gone away; they were only suspended in limbo during my hospitalization. Insecurity now started to set in again—for both of us.

The last week of my hospital stay, Anne never visited once. I covered this up with the family. She made the excuse that she was on the run, trying to get the home and trailer ready for my return so I would be comfortable. This was somewhat true, but was not the crux of the problem. She was still questioning her love for me, and it was driving her crazy. She called twice to tell me she was going to the movies with Ken, a new neighborhood friend who had been supportive. She said she had to get out of the house and needed space.

My insecurities were back, but deep inside I felt she loved me. After all, hadn't she shown it every single day of my hospitalization until the very last week? My insecurities also were partially blocked out by my tremendous desire and excitement about getting out of the hospital.

My last three days in the hospital were spent exercising, walking the wards, and visiting nurses, dieticians, and other patients and sharing with them the excitement of going home. My emphasis was on becoming physically strong. Only six days of my last 30 days in the hospital were spent up and around; the other 24 were flat on my back. It's amazing how your muscles deteriorate, become weak, flabby and saggy.

In my mind I figured I would return home, take three or four weeks of exercising, and then return to work.

Boy, was I wrong!

Somehow I still had not fully grasped the seriousness of my injuries. As most burn patients eventually realize, the road ahead was going to be long and hard and in some respects tougher than the pain and trauma of my initial hospitalization. And besides the physical issues, the road ahead was going to be full of social, economic, and psychological roadblocks.

I began to feel new anxieties about going home. The hospital had been my home for 70 days. It was a safe, clean, caring environment, one that had helped me survive. Now like the blindfolded person playing pin the tail on the donkey, they would blindfold me, spin me around three times and say, "Go to it! Go home! You're okay now." And like many blindfolded persons, burn survivors walk into walls, fall down, and get hurt in so many ways that the public isn't even aware of.

D-Day arrived. On Saturday, July 20, 1979, I was discharged from Peter Bent Brigham. Anne arrived with our beloved neighbor, John Resnik, at 10:00 A.M. For the first time in 70 days, I put on clothes. I was extremely excited about wearing a T-shirt and underwear. Nudity is somewhat more accepted inside the hospital walls, but it was still never comfortable and I was glad to be dressed again like other people!

I was given plenty of lanolin, gauze, ace bandages, support socks and miscellaneous supplies and medications. My bags were packed. The tears that filled my eyes were tears of joy, sadness of leaving, and tears of fear.

As I walked out the front door of the hospital my eyes squinted under the bright sunny July sky. Then I noticed a familiar object, my 1977 gray T-Bird, sparking clean, decorated with balloons, streamers, and banners that read "Welcome Home, George. You made it! You showed 'em!"

Driving off reminded me of our wedding day, but surely it was a different kind of excitement. Some other drivers tooted their horns; they weren't sure why; they only knew that it appeared to be a happy occasion. John sat in the back, Anne drove, and I rode shotgun.

Each mile brought new awareness. How clean and bright the day seemed, but I also noticed new physical awareness. My new thin skin was extremely sensitive to the clothing that now covered my body. I sweated profusely. Sixty percent of my sweat glands had been destroyed, which meant that the unburned skin now pushed body fluids at accelerated rates. My sensitive, painful ribs now acted as shock absorbers to every bump in the road. Throbbing returned to my legs, and fatigue quickly set in, but despite this, my mind was beyond my physical being. What did the house look like? How would I manage in a trailer? I couldn't wait to see my boys. I was filled with so many thoughts. I thanked God for giving me a second chance and the strength and will to survive this nightmare.

For two and a half months I had thoughts of only one thing: Survive, live, get better physically. To hell with business, marital problems, family problems, and day-to-day stresses and challenges. My body had responded. I gave it everything it asked for and then some. When it asked for rest, I gave it rest. When asked to exercise, I did more than required. When my body called for 8,000 calories a day, I gave it 10,000. I gave the only life and the only body I have 120 percent effort every day. I played to win. I always play to win. And somehow I kept my humor and stayed positive. I believed in living and wanted to live.

The car rounded the bend, just a couple hundred more yards to home. A 20-foot banner stretched over the driveway reading "Welcome Home, George." Another banner was on the garage; "We Love You," it read. Many of the same friends and neighbors who had witnessed the horror of the fire 70 days ago were on the scene again.

Had this happened only 10 short weeks before? Could he be home already? Many didn't believe it.

My hunched-backed body shuffled out of the car. I choked back tears. Stephen and David gingerly hugged me and told me they loved me amid many tears of joy.

My eyes scanned the yard. A 30-foot gray and white metal trailer propped on blocks sat in the backyard. There were signs of reconstruction with new lumber and building materials surrounding the house. Traces of smoke damage and charred timbers remained; there were soot-stained bricks over my escape door at the front of the house.

My mind was again beyond my exhausted throbbing body. Somehow I heard Anne say, "Come on. Let's not overdo it. You need to lie down and rest."

But I insisted on going inside the house. There were no traces of fire, only signs of new construction, plywood floors, new cabinets, like a new home three weeks from completion. How extensive had this fire been? I didn't know how much I had blocked out. Our home had been gutted top to bottom, stripped to the outside walls. It would take $80,000 worth of insurance money to return the house to livability.

Somehow I made it into the trailer. I feebly thanked everyone and said I had to rest. I collapsed on a bed that had been set up for me in the living room. I remember almost nothing about the rest of the day.

18

Sunday morning brought new revelations and challenges. Such a simple thing as a shower was more difficult than I had anticipated. I'll just jump in, clean up and relax, I thought. No way! My newly grafted skin and second degree scars were not only sensitive to clothing but extremely sensitive to the water beads from the showerhead. Each drop smarted, feeling like a pin prick. I couldn't stand it. I immediately set the plug and started to fill the tub.

Without the ace bandages on my legs, they started to puff, throb and swell. The deep red coloring immediately turned to purple. Poor circulation was the main reason. Cells, vessels, nerve endings, and sweat glands had been destroyed or partially damaged. Tremendous healing was still going on. I was very leery of slipping and falling. Somehow I managed to sit down in the tub. Taking the weight of my 190-pound frame off my lower legs brought great relief.

I could barely touch my skin with a washcloth. I felt weak and tired already. It was now time to get out of the tub. I braced myself on each side of the tub. Heave ho! Nothing happened. Heave ho! Nothing happened again. My arms, which once could do 50 push-ups per day and swing a decent tennis racket, were now weak and limp. My muscles had deteriorated more than I could imagine.

I called out for Anne. She wasn't there. She must have been busy in the house answering the numerous questions of electricians, plumbers, carpenters, painters, and wallpaper hangers. She had become our general contractor. She focused so much of her energies on this work in part because she was running from the reality of our broken relationship. She couldn't cope with my being home, with my physical condition and my scars, with whatever might lie ahead for us.

I started to panic. How will I get out of this tub? Relax and rest, I thought. Maybe she'll be here soon. I closed my eyes to rest; then I panicked. Maybe I'll pass out and drown. That thought pumped adrenaline through my body. My arms quivered. I turned on one side and kneeled up. I was sweating already. I slowly stepped out of the tub, the trailer tub offered a long step to the floor below and my legs buckled. I almost fell. This was one time I was glad the walls were very close.

Just toweling off my body also caused pain and discomfort; soft towels now seemed like sandpaper to my burned areas. I gingerly made it to the bed again. How long would it be like this? It suddenly hit me how weak I truly was. I would need lots of therapy and exercise. I had to come up with a program.

When Anne returned I told her the story of my bath. It shocked her into realizing that I was going to need some help physically.

My mind now seemed to be cluttered with new fears. Where did I fit in as a parent? How long would it be before Anne and I would have sex? Where was this troubled marriage going? These thoughts coupled with my physical problems set my head spinning. While in the hospital I was only worried about me. Now I had to worry about a marriage and the children.

I decided that to be strong physically was my top priority. I would not push the other issues and questions. Two days went by quickly. I found myself sleeping a lot, but I took two walks daily. I had to put ace bandages on my legs, long sleeve shirts, a sun hat with a large visor, and sunscreen lotion on my face. My new enemy was the bright July sun; it could wreak havoc with my skin. A short 50-yard walk to the house and back to the trailer proved this to me. My nose turned bright red, and the scars around my eyelids and chin quickly reddened and became more obvious. I knew I had to be careful. I would have to exercise early in the morning and early evening.

My solitude was interrupted one morning by a feeble knock at the trailer door. I responded, "Come it."

An elderly gentleman, possibly 70 years old, stepped in. There was a brief silence. His face showed concern, compassion, and love as he quickly scrutinized me.

"Hello, Mr. Pessotti. My name is Byron McDonald. I live down the road."

Right away the light clicked on and tears filled my eyes.

"Come in; sit down. I'm so happy to meet you. Thank you so much for the inspiring letter you sent me in the hospital." I couldn't express my gratitude quickly enough.

Byron said, "I saw the Welcome Home banner, and something inside me said I have to stop and meet you. I didn't know whether you would throw me out, cry, or shout. I didn't know what to expect of you physically or emotionally."

As most burn survivors know, we possess an immediate bond. Only other burn survivors can relate to the pain and trauma of a fire. One of the first questions we often ask each other is how did you get burned. Byron explained that three years ago he struck a match to light his pipe; a spark dropped between his sweatshirt and an oriental shirt he wore underneath. The shirt was flammable. Suddenly he felt a burning sensation all over his chest. By the time he removed his shirt and sweatshirt, he had suffered second and third degree burns over the upper portion of his torso.

I could see the pain on his face as he told his story; tears streamed down his cheeks. He told me that he had never met another burn survivor that he could talk to. He lived alone and faced many questions and problems alone. There was no group for burn survivors to turn to, a group of former patients that maybe could share problems, experiences, successes, or failures together. I wondered why. Byron and I split a beer and he left. His visit meant so much to me; it was inspiring to see a recovered burn survivor.

People who didn't even know me offered help and support. Two days later another knock came at the trailer door. In stepped a man and his daughter, who I guessed was about six years old. She said, "Mr. Pessotti?"

"Yes."

"You have two sons. I thought that they must have lost all their toys in the fire. I told my Dad that I have this extra game that I don't use too much. Is it okay if I leave it for them?"

I never thought a six-year-old could speak so eloquently or bring me to tears. I was inspired by her thoughtfulness.

19

Each morning I could hear the rat-a-tat-tat of the carpenters' hammers. Thank God for insurance, something we all hate to pay because we think we will never need it. With rapidly appreciating real estate values, our home was almost underinsured, but, fortunately, we had enough coverage to rebuild. Each day as part of my exercise, I walked through the house. There was no trace of the fire, just the clean smell of fresh paint and new carpet.

I walked slightly hunched. My arms were bowed like boomerangs; I couldn't straighten them. I looked like a gorilla! Scar tissue was now starting to thicken and tighten. I didn't yet know that it took six to 12 months for scars to form. My red smooth scars now turned into thick bumpy lumps called keloids. I was also developing hypotrophic scarring, as well as quickly adding new words for my burn vocabulary.

Soon the ridges and thickness of the keloids was quite pronounced. My elbows were extremely tight. I couldn't wait for the Jobst sleeves, pants, and vest that had been ordered for me. These tight elastic garments had been tailored to fit me; they would act like another layer of skin, keeping smooth, even pressure on the scars. This would help the ridges, bumps, and clusters of Keloid tissue.

The day the Jobst clothing arrived, I couldn't wait to try them on. They were so tight that huge water blisters were created underneath this new intruder. Like a saddle, the Jobst garments would slowly break the runaway wild stallion scars. Within weeks I saw a difference. Each day the garments became easier to put on. In time they were like underwear; I wouldn't be caught without them.

The kids were slowly adjusting to my return home. They seemed very protective of me, being careful not to bump into me. They quickly learned how sensitive my skin was. They had missed our private bedtime conversations and storybook reading. In a limited way I was trying to be a father. It became clear that my absence had created discipline problems.

Anne had tried her best to be a mother and father; she had visited me daily, coordinated rebuilding the home, picked appliances, listed lost items for insurance purposes, and held up the spirits of relatives and friends. She was tough on the outside and a marshmallow on the inside. Internally, she was hurting more than I knew. Why us, she wondered. Why George? What did he ever do to deserve this? But, most of all, some inner conflict made her question her love for me. She somehow couldn't or wouldn't love me, and, as a result, she was experiencing tremendous guilt feelings.

Anne was on Valium. She suffered from hypertension and couldn't sleep nights. With my return home, the pressure of being a wife was building. She made excuses that she couldn't sleep with me because of the sticky, greasy Lanolin that was rubbed all over my body, twice a day. This was true, but internally I began to question her rationalization. I tried to be patient. I tried to understand.

John Resnik, our neighbor across the street who took Anne and the kids into his home for three weeks, confided in me one day. One evening after Anne and the kids had moved into the trailer, John heard screaming across the street. He looked out the door and there was Anne, kneeling on the front lawn's burnt grass where my body had come to rest only weeks before. She was beating the ground with a tennis racket, crying and screaming uncontrollably.

"I'll put the flames out, George," she screamed. "I'll put them out. Why you? No, this didn't happen."

John ran to her and comforted her. Anne told him that as she was walking out of the house, she noticed a shredded piece of my shirt lying on the ground. It drove her into a frenzy. There were so many roadblocks and red flags that made her relive the fire daily. Her nightmares were frequent. After hearing John's story, I told myself to be more patient and understanding. Day by day the seriousness of this whole tragedy and its long-lasting impact on me and the people around me slowly become more evident.

I began to step up my exercise program. Each day I struggled to my knees and tried to put pressure on my arms. The arms that once could knock off 50 push-ups now struggled to do one. Day by day a little strength returned. My walking exercise slowly turned into a fast walk and within two weeks turned into a jog. Within two weeks I was jogging a mile. As I ran, sweat poured off my body; my unburned areas pushed fluid profusely. The legs and grafted areas oozed blood and muck. My ace bandage would stick to the grafts as I peeled them off. I was getting stronger. I was healing. I was alive again.

Neighbors, family, and friends marveled at me but encouraged me not to overdo it. How could I ever thank these people for their help and support?. I told Anne I'd like to throw a big party and thank everyone. We started planning a big bash for August 26. We invited the entire Police Department, the Fire Department, the ambulance crew, neighbors, friends, and family.

20

The house was now completed. Anne told me that next morning she had to go the bank in Worcester to pick up the final insurance check. Another milestone, I thought. Now we could settle down as a family again. My dreams were short-lived.

I was resting comfortably in bed when I heard a car pull in. It was Leo, the insurance agent, and Anne returning from the bank. They went into the house to check things out. In five minutes they returned. Leo climbed into the car, and Anne leaned in the driver's side door. I watched and listened. I heard Anne say in a sharp, crisp voice, "Don't say that; it makes me angry."

I thought, "What the hell did he say to her?" I was concerned when Anne returned. I immediately questioned her. I could tell by her nervous look that I had put her on the spot.

"What did Leo say that upset you so much?"

"Nothing. I don't know."

I exploded, "What do you mean you don't know? It was only three minutes ago! How could you forget? I know if I told someone, 'Don't say that; it makes me angry,' I would remember the comment."

She said nothing.

Suddenly all my insecurities returned. "Is there something going on between you and Leo?" I asked.

Again, no reply.

"Well, tell you what, you think about what I said, and when you are ready, I will expect the truth."

All day I thought and wondered what he said. Why was she lying? Anne had told me what a super job Leo had done on the insurance work. He had been there daily, counting dirty sooty clothes and personal items piece by piece.

Unknown to Anne, Leo had become very fond of her. Much later she told me that upon returning from the bank, Leo had sprung it on her; he told her that he loved her. She was flabbergasted! She was so weak emotionally, but she was also flattered.

But that evening, she only said, "Leo said good-bye to me and told me his work was done. She said she got upset when he said good-bye and she commented, "Don't say that; it makes me angry." Good try, but I knew it wasn't the truth.

How insecure I felt. Where would I go now if our marriage fell apart? I was not well physically. My physical and emotional needs weren't being met.

I had flashbacks of our two separations, one that lasted about two weeks and one that was for four months. During the first separation I had tried to keep the situation from my family, especially my parents. Not knowing where to go, I would drive around looking for an affordable motel each night, sometimes ending up far down I-95 near the Rhode Island border. I would call my parents and tell them I was on the road, so they wouldn't call the house and wonder why I wasn't there. During the second separation, I lived in a rooming house in Quincy, near work. It was very depressing.

During that longer separation, the warm friendship I had enjoyed with my secretary, Joanne Sparks, had gradually turned to romance. This happened after we went to lunch one day and she confided that she was having second thoughts about her upcoming wedding to the man who was to be her second husband. She had found out that he had lied to her about his job and about his credit card debt. But the wedding invitations had gone out, and her parents had already bought her a wedding gift. She was feeling a lot of stress about making the right decision.

As a friend, I advised her that she had three choices: She could marry the guy, she could postpone the wedding and look into these issues that were causing her to have doubts, or she could break up with her fiancé.

The next day, Joanne didn't show up for work. When I asked another woman in the office about her whereabouts, she said, "Whatever you said to her yesterday at lunch helped her make a firm decision. She broke up with her fiancé last night; the wedding is off!"

Another evening some weeks later, after my relationship with Joanne had become much closer, I asked her when her birthday was.

"March 19," she said.

"What year?" I asked.

"1950."

Apparently, my face turned a funny shade.

"Did I say something wrong?" Joanne asked.

"No, no, not at all."

"Well, you look awfully funny."

After much more pleading from Joanne, I finally admitted that she and Anne had been born on the same day in the same year.

"Where were you born?" I then asked.

"Boston Lying-in Hospital."

I couldn't believe it. Joanne and Anne had been born in the same hospital on the same day!

Although Joanne and I were developing deep feelings for one another, I eventually decided that, for the sake of the children, I had to return home to my family. I had been brought up to believe that, for better or worse, you stick it out in a marriage and do everything you can to make it work. Plus, I wasn't used to failing at anything, let alone something as important as this.

But now, with my return home from the hospital, pressure again was building on the marriage. I knew we were headed for a collision. No one in the family knew the truth; only a few close friends knew there were problems. We were spending money left and right restoring the house. The thought crossed my mind, we're acting like a married couple, but in reality we're not.

The collision soon came in early August. I had only been home three weeks. Anne and I sat in the new home, having a cocktail. I asked her, "Do you love me? Do you want to stay married? Have you made a decision?"

She couldn't hide it anymore and broke down.

"I don't know why, but I don't think I love you. Your hospitalization gave me time to think... time to make a decision."

I reminded Anne that I had previously told her if the day came when she told me she didn't love me, I would leave.

The timing seemed so terrible. I started planning my departure. I needed time to heal more physically. We discussed the party. I still wanted to go through with it. Our marriage difficulties had no bearing on my desire to thank all these people.

The day of the party proved to be one of the toughest emotional days of my life. August 26 was a bright sunny day. A big tent was pitched in the backyard. The garage was set up as an open bar with every liquor you could name. I hired three bartenders and a caterer. There was barbecued chicken, clam chowder, corn on the cob, salads, breads, and pastries. What a feast.

People came from near and far to celebrate this joyous occasion. George was home alive, in his new home.

If they only knew! How could I face these people? This may be the last day I would see many of them as a married man. The pressure was overwhelming. Many friends and family that couldn't see me in the hospital came and expressed their love and concern. Maureen, the new friend and burn patient I met in the hospital, drove with her mother from Worcester to see me. She had made the long trip lying down in the back seat to rest.

I walked around in a daze with such heavy, mixed emotions. Somehow the day passed. I was resting my swollen legs on a footstool when my brother-in-law came in and said, "It's time for us to go."

David was always staunch, straight forward, and firm, and he very rarely showed his feelings. We were close; he and his wife, Penny, had visited me faithfully in the hospital. Dave looked me straight in the face. His eyes watered, and his voice quivered.

"George, I'm so proud of you. You showed me so much courage in the hospital. I've learned so much from you. I love you." A tear ran down his cheek and he turned and walked away. I struggled to hold back my tears. I choked and pretended I was resting.

Joanne arrived with a friend. She was always there for me. We were the best of friends. Joanne was the only one at the party that day who read my face and understood the true emotions there. She looked at me and knew my marriage was over. Our closeness had taught us to read each other's feelings and emotions.

Physically and emotionally exhausted, I collapsed into the double bed in the upstairs guestroom after the party. A few days passed. I continued to exercise faithfully. My head was again spinning. Could this marriage really be over? My role as a full-time parent would soon be reduced to a part-time father. Hurt physically, I now had to deal mentally with a broken heart. My physical and mental body was being taxed to its limits.

New fears set in. Where would I live? When could I return to work? How would family and friends react to this? Would they again show their love, be supportive and understanding as they had in the past? How much can one's love take and how long will it endure? Does love have patience? Does it endure forever?

Who could I talk to? I felt trapped. I couldn't drive; I couldn't get away. This forced me to focus on the physical me. It drove me to exercise harder, endure more pain, stretch, bend, do pushups, jog, get strong. But each day the emotional me would compete for attention; it was hurting; it wanted time. I tried not to give in to it.

Anne and I began the painful conversation about how we would do this.

Does this mean we can now date other people? What do we do financially? When would I leave? What about visitation rights, holidays, children's education, insurance, dividing equity, furniture?

Our entire eight years of marriage was reduced to a piece of paper and a list of items. How impersonal that eight years of your life ends by the husband mailing a check each week to his ex-wife. We decided to work for an amicable divorce with no bitterness. We would try to remain friends and not alienate the children from either parent. We would each ensure them of our love for them. The amicability would be fine until the attorneys got involved. They played games, they dealt the cards, they carved the pie, they showed little compassion, and, oh yes, they got paid handsomely.

21

The answer as to when and how I would leave came sooner than expected. Yes, we did agree that we would go our separate ways, but I never expected Anne to have a date the next night!

Somehow within my menagerie of pain and suffering, I managed to find a small element of pride.

"If you're going out," I said, "I will not stand for a stranger to come to my house, pick up my wife, and take her to dinner. You leave, you meet him somewhere."

Anne's first night out would prove to be an eternity. My emotional me conquered my physical me. I lay in bed crying for a long time. I had held back the tears for so long. I needed a good cry; I owed myself one.

The hours clicked on. My tears were interrupted by Stephen, standing in the doorway, all of five years old.

"Why are you crying, Dad? Where's Mom? I want Mom."

Somehow Stephen knew I needed him. He hugged me close and patted me on the back as I wept like a baby. He sensed something was drastically wrong. How much can a child endure...the pain of seeing me aflame, visiting me in the hospital, and now this—"Dad will be leaving soon." How unfair. I felt so cheated. I reassured Stephen that I was okay and that Mom would be home soon. I tucked him back into bed, and, as children do, he quickly fell back to sleep.

My solitude, thoughts, and tears were interrupted by the sound of a car door slamming. It was 2:00 A.M. Anne was home. I had so much to say. As she tiptoed to the top of the stairs, I opened up on her.

"How could you be out with another man? If you think I'm going to lie here and suffer physically and mentally and baby-sit your kids while you go out with someone else, I won't stand for it. I'm leaving. If I have to crawl out of here, I will before I'll stand for these shenanigans."

Where I would go, I didn't know, but I knew one thing for sure. I was leaving. Hurt can't be measured on a scale of one to ten, but if it could, this hurt would be a 15.

I no longer could figure Anne out. She was no longer predictable. In her own world, she was hurting tremendously. She was carrying so much guilt over this decision that many times she acted without thinking. I knew her actions were not deliberate attempts to hurt me. She was possessed by her own problems. She could no longer deal with my issues and hers at the same time. Agree with her behavior or not, she was fighting for her own survival, too.

I've always respected people for making firm decisions, whether I liked the decisions or not. At least you know where you stand with these people. Firm decisions waste the least amount of our most precious commodity, time. We have only one life to live, so let's get on with it.

Breaking the news to others would not be easy. My close-knit loving family would react, grieve, hurt, and experience pain, but not at my level. They would make judgments about Anne. I had to be careful about how to explain it. Anne knew she would face tremendous rejection by my family as well as hers, for I was well loved.

I rehearsed my lines. I had to tell my parents. I desperately needed some love, some support, someone to talk to. I invited them over one evening. Anne had left the house. I made the excuse that she was playing tennis. But my parents suspected something was up. They were more observant than I thought. Disappointments over the years had conditioned them to be more understanding, to be more tolerant. My father's heart attack, the fire, and other family divorces had taught my parents that life is not always as predictable as we'd like it to be.

I struggled with what to say and how to say it. I knew that once I started the conversation the words would come easier.

"Mom and Dad, I have something to tell you. Anne and I are getting divorced. We were having problems prior to the fire; we were separated twice. We've seen marriage counselors, priests, and psychiatrists, and it's just not working."

They weren't as shocked as I expected.

"We've suspected so for a while," Mom said.

"How did you know?"

Mom confided that there was a slip of the tongue one night while they visited the Resniks. Mom had made a comment that I had sure been through a lot, and John said, "Yeah, Anne has sure put him through a lot of shit."

Mom said, "We saw other things—your expression, your tone of voice, your infrequent visits, and so on."

Overall, Mom and Dad were loving, understanding and supportive. I felt so relieved. I now had someone to talk to and share my fears with.

Anne arrived home that evening around 11. She was naturally anxious to see how my parents had reacted to the news of the divorce. I told her Mom and Dad had handled the news better than I expected. They were sorry and hurt, but most of all they were supportive and understanding.

I told Anne that for some time they had suspected we were having problems. She quickly asked what had made them suspicious. I explained that one evening John made a comment that she had put me through a lot of shit.

"He what? How could he! That no-good traitor! He said he would not repeat things I told him in confidence. That no-good bastard!"

Anne was livid. Of course the several gin and tonics she had had only added fuel to the fire. "I'm going to tell him what I think," she raged.

Anne was always outspoken and when something was on her mind, she'd let you know right away, no procrastination. I tried to calm her, but to no avail.

"I'm going over there and tell him what I think," she said again. Luckily, the Resniks weren't home.

"I'm waiting up for him," Anne said with determination in her voice.

"Look, don't do anything you'll be sorry for. You're too angry. Wait and talk to John one-on-one; your beef is with him, not the whole family. I don't want you waking up his whole family."

At this point the only thing that made sense to Anne was that she was hurt and John would hear about it. I was now getting angry, but her anger was far greater than mine.

At midnight John's car pulled in driveway. It was now time for the shoot-out. Anne ran out of the house with both barrels blazing. "John, you liar, you no good Judas bastard. How could you betray me? I trusted you!"

John quickly ran across the street. They met eye to eye, toe to toe.

"What are you talking about? How dare you call me a bastard!"

"You told George's parents about all the shit I put him through. How could you?"

John vehemently denied it and ran home shouting and cursing. By this time, most of the lights were on in the neighborhood! Nobody got much sleep that night.

The repercussions of this shouting match lasted for several weeks. It seemed so strange not having the Resniks visit on a daily basis. They had always been so supportive. In many respects they were also victims. Because of the fire, they were suddenly very involved in our lives—and our problems–much as though they were part of our immediate family. But time does heal most wounds, including emotional ones. Within three weeks Anne and John half apologized to each other, and much of the tension went away.

22

I made a decision to leave home by October 1. I always lived up to my commitments. I now had to be concerned about finances. How much could I spend for rent, food, clothing, and so on? It was a totally new experience. A friend of mine offered me a bedroom in a penthouse condominium on Atlantic Avenue on Boston's waterfront. It sounded okay. It would be a start, a resting place, a way station, a place to build up steam to go forward.

As the days clicked by in September each one brought increasing pressure. Pressure to leave Anne, whom I still loved, Stephen and David, my home, my family, my friends. So much would change.

Try to explain to a five-year-old and a three-year-old that their Dad, who they hoped so much would live after a terrible accident, was now going away. Night after night at bedtime I choked through the kids' prayers. Bedtime was a special time, a time for prayers, stories, and warm conversation.

One night, Stephen asked, "Dad, when you leave home, will it be forever?"

"Steve, I don't know. I think so."

"I don't want you to leave; I'll miss you."

"Me, too!"

"Dad, when you were in the hospital, you said you were coming home forever. Why are you leaving? Is it because of the fire?"

So many hard questions with impossible answers. I realized that children have such special needs; they have feelings and are entitled to honest answers. Many times my sons' anger was expressed by breaking toys, by disobeying, by being plain ornery to get back at me for letting them down.

I remembered the things Dad did with me—playing catch, attending Little League games, basketball games, sporting banquets, so many things that all of a sudden shocked me into understanding parenthood. How could I give Steve and Dave all these things on a part-time basis?

Life seemed so cruel. We were all victims of the fire and the divorce, each struggling to survive and find our place in life. I continually told my boys that I loved them, that they were not the reason for the divorce, and that I would always be there for them.

Now came the painful task of sorting out the divorce. How much does Anne get each week? Will the house be sold? Who gets what furniture? Who pays for college, insurance, orthodontia work, summer camp—the list seemed endless. Such important issues to answer under so much pressure.

Finally, the day I was to move out arrived. Part of me felt my life was ending that day. I had struggled and survived the fire, certainly enough pain and trauma for one lifetime, and now my family and marriage had fallen apart. I scurried around the house packing underwear, Lanolin, miscellaneous supplies. There was not much clothing to pack; almost everything had been lost in the fire.

The kids were clinging and asking, "When will I see you, Dad?"

I found so much pain in these questions. Anne was crying, out of sadness, out of guilt, out of fear, and out of loss. All good reasons for tears, I suppose. I struggled to hold back my own tears, but they ran down my cheeks like a car sliding on ice. My lips moved but no sound could be heard. I searched for something to sum up all this agony. What could I say? I mumbled "Goodbye." It was such a small word but so powerful, for this word broke my heart.

I turned and walked away. I couldn't look back; it was too hard. I scuffled my body to the car, alone again. The Welcome Home banner no longer hung from the garage. I was not home anymore. I was leaving.

As I drove away the tears fell so effortlessly, so unending, so bizarre, eight years of my life consisted of a color TV and a suitcase. Is that all there is? The ride to Boston was a blur. I arrived and quickly fell asleep, emotionally and physically drained.

23

The next morning brought much newness. The day was so quiet and lonesome. The familiar voices and questions of the children were missing. No one was there to help me physically. The companionship of neighbors was absent and sorely missed. The encouragement to get better would now have to come from within.

Being married one often takes much for granted, food in the refrigerator, clean laundry, clean sheets, ironed shirts and so on. Now I realized I had to do all of these things myself. Maybe I noticed much more because I was weak physically. Every chore became a task. Groceries had to be held in my aching, weak arms while the elevator traveled 10 stories. Parking the car in Boston also required so much effort.

Even though I was alone most of the time in the condo, I felt it was not home. It was not my furniture, dishes, or supplies. The atmosphere was bright, lots of plants, lots of glass, and a spectacular view of the city and Boston Harbor. One day I sat with a telescope watching Logan Airport and the ships of the harbor. Airliner after airliner taxied and blasted off. Oil tankers, barges, tugs, cruise ships, fishing boats...there was so much interesting activity to watch! It made me miss my work.

I loved meeting people and selling real estate. My mind became preoccupied with at least driving to the office a couple of days a week. Opening mail, returning some phone calls, possibly keeping my mind occupied. I phoned the office to let them know I would be stopping by for a few hours. I was so excited; I couldn't wait to see old faces and to thank everyone for the many cards.

The next morning I realized that this was the first time in six months that I was dressing up for something. But the process wasn't easy. Crawl out of bed; do 20 minutes of stretching exercises to fight off the stiffness and tightness I felt each morning; take a shower that seemed to last forever because the drops still felt like pellets against my sensitive skin; dry off with a towel, a process that took so long that my arms were heavy and could barely reach my face to shave; rub Lanolin over my entire body; slide the Jobst elastic sleeves on both arms; put on support socks; pick a light shirt that wouldn't rub my painful and sensitive ribs. By this time, my heavy arms struggled to button my top button. I couldn't do it; my arms wouldn't bend enough.

It took a full two hours to get dressed and ready. I was exhausted. How could I make it through a day at the office? I slowly weaved my car through the city to the Southeast Expressway. I was nervous, afraid I wouldn't react in time to traffic and Boston's many obstinate, impatient, inconsiderate drivers.

Finally I arrived at the office, 20 minutes away in Braintree. I regrouped my thoughts and memories. Was I really back? As I entered the building and saw the familiar faces, I quickly felt at home. So many handshakes, smiles, friendly comments, conversations, and, of course, concerned looks.

People were naturally curious about what I would look like. Fortunately, my clothes hid most of my scars. My hands still turned purple, and redness around my nose, eyes, and neck hinted that something had happened, but most people knew very little about what I had experienced in the last six months.

For the next two months I found myself repeating the details of the accident many times. Thank God I could talk about it with candor. So many burn survivors withdraw because they can't handle the questions, can't accept their accident yet, and can't face the social ramifications of scarring and the stares from people.

I learned that most people mean no harm when they stare or ask questions. They're simply curious; they want to know what happened to you for different reasons. Some people thrive on gossip and gory details; it gives them something to talk about. Too often, people ask burn survivors personal questions that are hard to answer. Some people grab you and slap you on the back, not knowing they could be causing you pain. Some stare without realizing it. Some brush off your injury as if it were nothing. I think the public could well use an education course on how to deal with people who have been hospitalized, burned, or otherwise absent from society for a period of time.

I was happy to return home that afternoon. I learned I would have to pace myself physically. I needed a nap every day. I had to care for myself. No one else would look out for me; I had to care for number one.

I now had to deal with new family routines and priorities. My commitment to the children was to see them every Wednesday afternoon and every Saturday. Every other weekend they would stay over one night. The time I now spent with the children was quality time. I realized that when I was married, many times I was going through the motions. I'd arrive home from the office, Anne and the kids would say hello and I wouldn't really hear them because my head was still spinning from the day at the office. I would think about the business calls I had to make that evening. If I settled down to read the paper, the kids would be joking, playing, and fooling around. Many times I would say, "Don't bother me; I'm tired," or "Don't bother me; I'm reading. I'll play with you in a while. Don't bug me," and the other classic lines for poor parenting. Weekends I did chores and errands. I was around the kids, but I was only going through the motions; I wasn't spending quality time with them.

Being divorced made me put a priority on my time with the boys. I penciled in special time for the kids, no business, just one-on-one time. We went fishing together. Oh, the joy of watching Stephen cast his rod for the first time, the excitement on catching his first fish, digging worms. I was a kid again, reliving my days as a child and enjoying it. We should never lose our childish excitement. Society conditions us not to laugh, not to smile, to act grownup. I never want to grow up!

I found my love for the kids growing each and every month. I couldn't wait for Wednesdays and Saturdays. I was enjoying myself and the kids. No business interference. I changed business plans so that my Wednesdays and Saturdays were always spent with the kids, something I had never done before the accident. They could count on me. They looked forward to our time. How quick they learned the days of the week. David would say on Wednesday, "When are you coming again, Dad?" If it was an overnight weekend I'd say, "Not tomorrow, but Friday." Their faces would brighten as they realized that wasn't so long.

We went skating, bowling, visited friends and family overnight, read stories, built tree houses and tire swings, went to the movies, the Children's Museum, the Aquarium, parks, and, yes, some days we did nothing.

24

Anne and I had decided our divorce would be different. We would not pit one parent against the other, as so many divorcing parents do. We would not divide our love and use our children as the whipping blocks for our problems. We would remain human, caring, and loving, but would go our separate ways. We would continue to communicate, talk about the kids' schooling and their emotional needs, and continually reassure them of our love. We would let them know that they were not the reason for our divorce.

For a long time the kids drew a correlation between the fire and our marriage breakup. So many times David, now 4 years old, would say, "Dad, I wish that fire never happened."

"Why, David?"

"Because I miss you. You were all burned. Your face looked like a monster in the hospital." He had vivid memories.

"Dad," he continued, "Why don't you live here any more? Why can't we do things as a family?"

In time their questions lost their intensity, but never, ever will they forget that fire.

Anne and I made a list of agreeable terms for our divorce. We agreed to split the house and all cash 50/50, divide furniture equally, and pay off all bills. I agreed to pay for insurance, college, camp and so on, plus send Anne a hefty weekly check.

Everything seemed agreeable. Now enter the monkey wrench, the adversary, the tyrant who makes his living on fees, the man who would rock the boat, upset the apple cart, the genius who would bring out hate, dissent, and animosity between Anne and me. Guess who! That's right, the divorce attorney.

All of a sudden Anne's attorney said, "Don't split the cash with George. We'll negotiate it and use it as a bargaining point."

"But, Mr. Attorney, I have to live and Anne has all the cash. I have no money for furniture, security deposits, clothing and living expenses."

Did he care? No.

"Don't split the house 50/50, Anne," he advised. "It should be 60/40, and

George should pay your legal fees. It's only $2,500."

Let's examine the logic here: Anne is divorcing me and I should pay her legal fees, plus my own attorney fees?

Thanks to Anne's attorney, peace turned to chaos. Friend became enemy. Why not one arbitrator to fairly represent both parties? Why tie up court time and let criminals go free because they can't get a speedy trial? Why lie about facts, create phony stories, have witnesses perjure themselves by saying your wife's an adulteress? Why? If your marriage is over, it's over. No need to waste the court's time by fabricating lies.

Living away from home, penniless, out of work, and in a lot of physical and mental pain, I became angry. I told Anne, "We agreed on 50/50 on cash. You know that's fair. I don't need any attorney in a three-piece suit telling me what's mine. I need it to live."

"Well, he advised me not to!" she responded.

"I don't care what he advised you. This is a moral issue for us."

This negotiating dragged on for six months, after which a 35-page divorce settlement was signed, and $5,000 was paid to two attorneys. The settlement was so detailed that if one of the kids broke a shoelace, I knew who would pay for a new one.

In the meantime, my temporary living quarters on the waterfront weren't working out well. My friend and his wife, owners of the condominium, unexpectedly returned to Boston. Their friends and company were coming in and out. I felt like a stranger living in someone else's home.

Who would ever think that Oreo cookies would cause me to move? The kids visited one weekend, and after I brought them home, I drove the long, lonely 50 miles back to Boston. On the kitchen counter, I found a snippy note: "Can't you keep this place a little cleaner. There were Oreo cookies all over the kitchen floor. Get the message."

This note really upset me. Obviously, it was time to look for a home of my own where no one would get upset by a few cookie crumbs. I couldn't afford to buy a home, so I decided to look for an apartment. Since my office was in Braintree, 12 miles south of the city, I figured it would be more convenient to live outside of the city when I was ready to return to work full-time.

I started checking the local paper for apartments and traveled up and down the highway, day after day looking at apartments. It reminded me so much of my two previous marital separations. Instead of calling a hotel or motel and hearing, "Sorry, we have no rooms available," the message I heard time after time was, "Sorry, this apartment has already been taken."

Finally a two-bedroom apartment was available in Weymouth, a large town next to Braintree. It was not the greatest apartment, but it was clean, so finally, on November 1, I had a place to call home.

It had been many years since college and my apartment days. I had forgotten so much. I realized it sure was a mistake letting Anne keep all the furnishings of our house. It could cost me literally thousands of dollars I didn't have to purchase the major pieces of furniture I needed to turn this small apartment into an acceptable home for the boys and me. But what about the minor items, wastebaskets, curtains, shower curtains, utensils, pots and pans, linens, light bulbs, detergents! My God, there were so many things to buy.

I decided to get the major items, at least a bed to sleep in. The incidentals took weeks. I did a little each day. My stamina was not yet up to snuff. I needed my daily naps. By Thanksgiving I was pretty well set up. By that time, I had no cash left, my lines of credit were fully borrowed, and my MasterCard was at its limit.

But what I did have was a second chance, a chance to live, a chance to turn my life around. Where did my strength, positive attitude, my faith, my never-ending desire not to quit, and to not to let up come from? Had God punished me enough; had he tested me enough? I proved to Him my life was worth living. I carried my cross, and miraculously, like the phoenix bird, I was reborn. Why did I survive? Did he have a purpose for me? So many prayers had been answered. So many friends and family asked him to spare me. Thank you, God, for listening, for answering those prayers.

25

I decided I would go to the office for a few hours three or four days a week. There was so much paperwork and so many phone calls to return. My immediate concern was the financial stability of the company. I now started remembering business details.

Right before the fire, I had been planning an open house on Martha's Vineyard; we were kicking off a new subdivision of 35 lots. My goal had been to sell out the entire subdivision that day. It was high goal, a lot to expect, but I had always set high goals, high standards. The tent had been ordered, the caterer was bringing chicken, clam chowder, lobsters, watermelon. We always put on a bash. Over 150 people were expected at the open house.

After my accident, my partner, Dick Valentine, Joanne, my close friend Dick Pratt, and others all pitched in. The open house was held, but some of the clients, who in many cases were also friends, quickly asked about my whereabouts. Dick Valentine made a short speech.

"May I have your attention, please? George is not here with us today. I'm sorry to say that he's in the hospital. A gasoline explosion last week burned him severely. He sends his apologies and hopes to return home soon. Your prayers and cards would be most appreciated."

At first there was a total hush, followed by quiet conversations as people tried to digest this news. Despite the gloom, my clients and customers responded. Twenty-seven of the 35 lots were sold. These sales helped carry the company financially for several months.

Our company had also been in the midst of a modest home building program that appeared to be going well at the time of my accident. Yet now, months later and despite the sales of the open house, my accountant informed me that the company was in a serious negative cash flow position. Somehow construction costs were drastically over budget. We were showing a $60,000 loss!

I was shocked. I couldn't believe it. What had happened? What went wrong? Bruce, my general contractor, offered no sensible explanations. I had to find out what went wrong. I became obsessed with this problem. Could my company go bankrupt? God, no, how would I live? Where would my salary come from?

I started to panic because I wasn't capable of selling yet. I was still getting tired mentally and physically. Dick Valentine reassured me everything would be okay. I later found out he had personally loaned the company $30,000 to help pay my payroll and overhead during my absence.

I decided to check out these extraordinary losses. I compared the actual charges paid against the budgeted numbers for the newly built homes. An immediate red flag appeared. On one home the budget for the foundation costs was $3,000, while the actual paid charge was $6,000. I immediately thought it must be a duplicate charge. I called the cement company on Martha's Vineyard to check this invoice.

"Hi, Mr. Goodale," I began. "I see you charged us for 60 yards of cement on your October invoice. That foundation only calls for 30 yards of cement. Could you check this, please?"

"Hold on, I'll check it out. " Shortly he returned and said, "We poured two foundations that day, one at Lot 131 and one at Dick DeRoche's house, the state trooper in Edgartown."

"Dick DeRoches? He's not a client of ours. Who authorized this?"

"Bruce, your foreman."

My God, Bruce charged a friend's foundation to our account and we paid for it. How come he didn't reimburse us, I wondered. I didn't want to blow the whistle until I had more information.

I next stumbled onto an invoice on which we had overpaid a foundation laborer $600. I called him to ask him when we could expect our $600. He indicated he had paid it to Bruce. Our records showed no receipt of these funds. The laborer produced a cancelled check.

I then noticed that there was $2,400 spent for a washer, dryer, and dishwasher. This was incredibly high. I found a paid bill turned in by Bruce indicating he had paid for these appliances with his personal funds. Our accountant reimbursed Bruce for the $1,200. But when Bruce's check to the appliance company bounced, they re-billed us for $1,200 and unknowingly our accountant paid the bill. This fiasco had cost us $1,200!

I now had strong evidence of a pattern of fraud. We were getting screwed. I had to then check every minor detail.

As I sat at my desk, my mind wandered. How could Bruce do this to us? We had done so much for him. He had an apartment for next to nothing and a new van. We paid his phone bill, electric and other utilities and paid him $40,000 on contracts. Wasn't that enough? Why was he stealing?

Only a year before on Christmas Eve Bruce had been lying in a Cape

Cod hospital with a bleeding ulcer. We paid him every week while he was out of work, and I personally ran the job for six weeks until he was able to return to work. I had also personally paid for his vacation with me to Jamaica. He had always gone out of his way to accommodate me. It was a two-way street. So why was he doing this now?

My mental pain over the revelation that someone I had trusted and considered a friend was stealing from my company was complicated by physical pain. The scar tissue in my arms was stiffening and tightening. I could hardly bend my arms. My elbows were so sensitive against the hard desktop, I couldn't flex my arms to get the phone receiver to my ear. I had to continually move my arms to keep the circulation going. The blood would stagnate in my lower forearms, giving them a deep purple look. The scars on my fingers also turned purple. I didn't want to overwork and have a breakdown. I tried to be aware of my mental and physical limits on a daily basis, taking a little at a time.

I didn't want to let Bruce know that we were on to his embezzlements. I figured if he found out he would cover his trail. In the interim Bruce had located another property for us. We eventually purchased it and had planned to pay him a $10,000 commission as a finder's fee. He started to press us for his fee. We certainly didn't want to pay him until we knew the extent of his wrongdoing. Luckily, the Town Planning Board questioned the original approvals, and we ended up in litigation over the property. This gave us an excuse not to pay him.

Finally we had enough evidence and Bruce was confronted and fired as our contractor. He continued to insist he had done nothing wrong. He believed his own lies! We had evidence in black and white. We had cancelled checks and phony receipts. We had numerous witnesses ready to testify. Yet Bruce continued to profess his innocence.

I made more and more discoveries about the extent of Bruce's fraud. Oddly enough, this work, which became somewhat of an obsession, helped keep my mind away from the thoughts of divorce, physical pain, and my loneliness for the children.

I now started to analyze our summer rental account. Most out-of-state renters paid a deposit when they reserved their space and then paid the remainder in cash upon check-in. A couple of balance sheets didn't balance. One weekly rental showed only $300 paid of a $600 rental. Possibly the tenant forgot to pay. I called him in New York. He was very indignant!

"What do you mean, I didn't pay!" he yelled at me. "I paid the $300 balance due in cash to a blond, curly haired guy. I think his name is Bruce."

I apologized for the inconvenience. I knew now that I had to keep digging. My school days of accounting and auditing were paying off.

I decided to question all invoices that were marked paid and turned in for expense reimbursement. The first call was to Martha's Vineyard Furniture for a $300 dining room table receipt. The table was for the apartment we rented to Bruce.

"Hello, Mr. Cohen, this is George Pessotti at United Businessman's Realty," I said. "I'm calling to verify that you have been paid in full for the dining room table."

"Paid in full! Hell, I've never been paid anything. Bruce said he'd be back to pay us. That was four months ago."

Bruce never paid the bill but was reimbursed $300 for the table on his expense account.

I learned through some business acquaintances that we had been overcharged $2.00 per square yard for all carpet installations. The net result was that Bruce had his girlfriend's house totally re-carpeted at our expense.

One more discovery, although insignificant in dollar amount, aggravated me to the point of real fury. Our new rental manager had given Bruce $100 cash to pay the manager's first month's medical coverage. Bruce assured him that he would drop the payment at our office. Bruce knew that our manager's wife had contacted multiple sclerosis so having medical coverage was critically important. One day our manager came in with a stack of bills from the hospital and we checked our records. We had to tell him he had not been enrolled in our health plan.

"What do you mean no coverage? I gave Bruce my premium; didn't he turn it in?"

"We have no record of it."

I now knew that we were dealing with a professional thief. Although he was not an employee, he did represent us. Everyone knew Bruce; he was a likeable guy. Our reputation was good, so everyone expected they would be paid. It brought up an interesting point. Where does a company's obligation to pay stop? Should we be totally responsible for the acts of an individual who acted on our behalf?

Bills that we never knew about now started filtering in. We received a bill for $4,400 for antennas. The homeowners had never authorized the installation. Bruce just thought it would be nice if all the new homes had antennas. We again got stuck for the bill.

My friend Dick Pratt showed me a cancelled check for $200 payable to Bruce for a 1971 Chevy Dick was buying for his girlfriend. Bruce never delivered that car, but, guess what? Yup, he cashed the check!

My excavation engineer called me to ask if I knew why Bruce had charged $53 worth of lobsters to the engineer's gravel account. The light went on. Bruce had told me he footed the tab for my lobster and steak welcome home party. But again, he didn't pay; he simply charged it to the subcontractors.

A few weeks later I bumped into Bruce on the Martha's Vineyard. He had the unmitigated gall to ask when we would pay him his $10,000 finder's fee! He still insisted that he had done nothing intentional. I know knew he had to be sick in the head. I lambasted him verbally.

"Bruce, how could you? After all I did for you. You say you did nothing, but you're lucky I'm not a wild tempered Italian. I ought to take the tire iron out of the trunk and beat your goddam brains in. That's what you deserve, you no good bastard. The phony receipts, the state trooper's foundation, the dining room table, the missing rent, the unpaid health insurance, the car you never delivered. Do you want me to stop here? You sorry son of a bitch. You've done nothing, eh? Let me tell you something, you get in your car and go home. I want you to stare at yourself in the mirror for ten solid minutes, and then ask yourself if you've done anything wrong. I think you will find the answer. Now get out of here."

Bruce turned and left with tears in his eyes. I assumed that after conversation I would never hear from Bruce again. I was very wrong.

26

The word around the Island was that Bruce was furious about our refusal to pay him the finder's fee. I had told Bruce we would settle our differences over that in court. But long before the matter came to court, disaster hit again.

I walked into the office one morning and Joanne said, "Did you hear?"

"Did I hear what?"

"The house you and Dick own on the Island burned to the ground last night."

"Come on, you must be kidding."

The look on Joanne's face told me that she was definitely serious.

"The fire chief called Dick last night; they're investigating. They say it was definitely set."

Bruce was the likely suspect, but he was nowhere to be found. We didn't have any real proof, just a gut feeling. Bruce had told me he would get even with us.

Of course, the news of the fire touched me in a way that only I could understand. Anytime I hear of or see a fire, it stirs feelings inside me, feelings I will never forget. For most survivors of fire, the fire never dies; it continues to burn inside. You carry your memories and scars forever.

The house was a total loss, a torch job right to the foundation. I was certain that Bruce had chosen arson as his tool of vengeance specifically because it was bound to cause me the most anguish possible.

Dick and I had to fly to Martha's Vineyard to answer routine questions. A police bulletin was put out for Bruce; he was wanted for questioning. We wanted him to take a lie detector test.

The bad news was not over. I called our insurance agent to report the loss. Mr. Frye, our agent, said, "Is that the house that you and Dick own in West Tisbury?"

"No, it's the three-bedroom ranch we own in Edgartown."

"I don't have a policy on any Edgartown house. Maybe your prior agent still has that account."

During my hospitalization the company had transferred all our insurance to a new agent, Mr. Frye. Dick and I had owned two homes on the Island. The old agent sent a memo to Mr. Frye asking him to pick up coverage on our Edgartown house. Mr. Fyre assumed that the Edgartown house and the West Tisbury house were one in the same! Our coverage was cancelled on the Edgartown house, but we had never received a cancellation notice. Both agents were negligent, but we were in the middle.

I felt so unproductive. All my time at work was spent playing Sherlock Holmes. I questioned whether I still had the ability to sell. It had been so long. Had I forgotten the skills of my trade? I was depressed and couldn't seem to motivate myself, something I had never faced before. I had always been positive minded and self-motivated. But now I was having trouble digging down deep to pull myself up. I had been knocked down so many times. Should I get up and fight again? I wanted to, but couldn't seem to find the combination.

Work had always been a positive release for me, a place for recognition and accomplishment. I now dreaded going into the office. There were no sales coming in; the business was sinking farther and farther into debt. Could I turn it around? Would my partner file for bankruptcy? Would I ever sell again? These thoughts and fears possessed me.

When I went home at night I now had something else to ponder. My frustrations at work came out in more anger over my divorce. Unfortunately, I no longer had an outlet for this or any other anger. Work had always been my release. Tennis had been another release, but, of course, I couldn't play tennis. How could I vent my anxieties? I felt so lonely.

My friends, family, and children would become my salvation. The time I spent with the kids on Wednesdays and Saturdays was becoming better quality time. I enjoyed it so much. Every time I left the kids, it was difficult. I tried to be strong. I choked back tears many times as I drove away.

My personal time was now being spent with Joanne. She continued to keep her apartment in nearby Marshfield but was soon spending many nights with me in Weymouth as our relationship grew stronger. Joanne was so patient, so tolerant, and so understanding of my needs. She became my nurse and my wife. She always watched out for my best interests and backed me up in everything I did. I needed someone to be close to, to share my fears, joys, anxieties, and pain with, and Joanne was always there for me.

Night after night, day after day, Joanne took care of me physically, too. Countless back rubs, arm rubs, leg rubs, side rubs. Methodically, never complaining, she rubbed me down with Lanolin. Lanolin was like taking morphine. It temporarily relieved and softened my skin. It helped eliminate some discomfort and tightness. The rubbing was so relaxing. So many nights I tossed and turned, searching for a comfortable position. My ribs were now experiencing tremendous keloid scarring. To lie on my ribs or sides caused much pain. The scars were forming; they pushed up and bumped up causing great tightness. The sheets and blankets rubbing against my sides always caused discomfort. My God, would the day ever come when I would experience no pain?

Some days I was very depressed. I tried to figure out why. Many times I accepted the fact that constant pain was taking its toll on me. The unending sensations would catch up with me. I blocked out pain many times by trying for focus my thoughts on positive issues. I tried to convince myself that things would get better. I had paid my price. It was only a matter of time.

Burn survivors go through so many adjustments. We face a two-phased recovery. First comes the initial hospitalization, with its unending pain and suffering, the day-to-day dressing changes, the struggle to survive, to live, to get better, accept new changes, but, most of all, to return to normal living.

But the second phase of recovery brings as many problems and adjustments. Society and the burn survivor are not experienced enough to deal with problems, problems that only months ago didn't exist. If the second phase of recovery is not dealt with properly, then the burn survivor drops out of society. He or she turns to alcohol or drugs or becomes a recluse. The problems and pain of coping become overwhelming. At the time of my injury, other than seeing a shrink or a therapist, there were no programs for burn survivors and families.

Post-burn adjustments are both physical and mental. Sensitive healing skin now rebels at closing. Rough, course fibers rub against the skin, causing pain and irritation, so the burn survivor has to adjust to a new dress code of looser fitting clothing. Ugly scars become a problem so the victim tries to dress to cover up many scars. Society rejects scars; they're foreign and ugly. People don't want to look at them. The burn survivor not only has to deal with accepting his or her scarring, but also must deal with a society that isn't prepared to look at those scars.

Other adjustments include being extremely careful for bright sun or light. Burn survivors are very susceptible to sunburn. Sun screening lotion helps, but doesn't eliminate the rays. Blistering of healing skin due to sun exposure is quite common.

If the burn survivor is wearing Jobst elastic garments, these take adjusting to, also. The garments are tight and difficult at first to pull or slide over the sensitive scars and grafts. The garments do help because the thin elastic serves as another layer of skin. They hold down the scarring process, eliminate many bumps and ridges.

There are also the sensations and tingling to adjust to. For many months, and in some cases years, cells, tissue, nerve endings, and blood vessels are regenerating. Blood flow to healing areas often gets trapped. The trapped, unoxygenated blood turns the immediate area purple. This discoloring lasts for some time. On grafted areas the new skin is so thin that you can see vessels and arteries. We burn survivors have to be so careful of bumps and bruises. The new skin tears, bruises, and rips very easily.

For the survivors of major burns, the third and fourth degree burns have devastated important sweat glands. The new skin lacks porosity to push out body fluids. Water retention is quite common. The unburned skin areas become recipients for added sweat and water loss. These unburned areas push body fluids at greatly accelerated rates.

The burned areas now are sensitive to temperature changes. In my case, the New England climate of warm, often humid summers and frigid, damp winters raised hell with my skin. Humidity for a healthy person is a problem, but how about a burn survivor, with so many sweat glands destroyed? Healthy skin is like a thermostat; it monitors hot and cold, but for a burn survivor, the monitors are missing. Coldness creates so much tightness, cringing, and stiffness for the burn survivor.

Other physical ailments that are a nuisance are itching and flaking of skin. I've spoken to some burn survivors who itch for years. Scars are like a glacier; they move and form slowly. Instead of dragging rocks and gouging valleys, the scars drag the burn survivor through emotional peaks and valleys.

Before the fire, my hairy arms and legs were something I always took for granted. Now the hair was gone. Grafted skin never regrows hair because the follicles are permanently destroyed.

Thank God I was blessed with so much hair in other areas. I remember one time when my brother and I had an apartment; he was cleaning the bathroom and commented to me, "I don't think we should carpet the bathroom."

I innocently asked, "Why not?"

"Because the bathroom is wall to wall hair already!"

Exercising is crucial for burn survivors, but for many it's also very painful. For most people it is difficult to exercise in pain. As a result they become lazy, a condition that the wild scarring enjoys because lack of exercise gives the forming scar a chance to be free and become tight and ugly on its own. If you don't exercise, you lose out to the scars. They conquer areas of weakness. Joints in the arms, legs and shoulders become bridges for the scars to span; they cross right over the joints and cause webs. The webs and scars constrict and contract. The end result of not exercising means more surgery for burn survivors. A release or contractual release is formed to surgically remove the web-like scar tissue. A new skin graft replaces the old scarring. I can't emphasize how important my exercising was to me. Day after day I faithfully did my sit-ups, push-ups, and jumping jacks.

The opposite side of the physical recovery is the mental recovery. For most major burns this is the most deadly or dangerous form of recovery to deal with. Doctors can expertly help your physical body, but the human mind is quite different. The conscious and subconscious minds raise hell with the burn survivor.

The mental side of healing is quite different from patient to patient. Some patients may have been receiving psychiatric help at the time of their accident and this is postponed. If a burn survivor had emotional problems prior to the accident, then these problems don't go away. Instead, they become intensified because the scarring and related traumas add fuel to emotional problems.

Some patients are drug addicts or alcoholics searching for their place in life. Their accident interrupts their life. Some victims are normal Americans never expecting tragedy to strike them. Fire is a lot like death; we never think much about dying. We all think we are infallible.

Part of the psychological healing is accepting what has happened. Eliminate the guilt. Some victims carry the guilt of their accident for years. Possibly they question their carelessness that led to the accident. Others constantly question why me? Why did this have to happen to me? But when you do this, you're living in the past. Life is in the present, not the past. The past we can never change. We can only learn from it.

Many fire victims have their careers interrupted. The ugly scarring may even eliminate opportunities in certain lines of work. The hardest thing burn survivors deal with is change. People in general are unwilling to change, are very set in their ways. But for things or life to change, we have to change. We have to change and change does not come easy; it takes

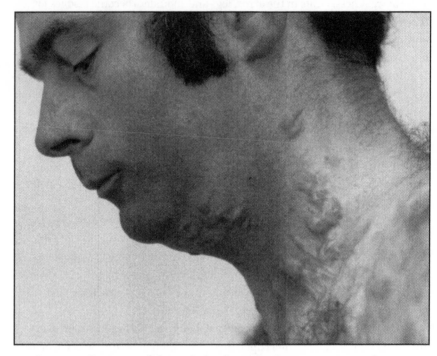

After a year, George was fighting the battle against the intense scarring that accompanies major burns. The keloid scars on his neck limited his ability to turn his neck from side to side, necessitating surgery to relieve this problem.

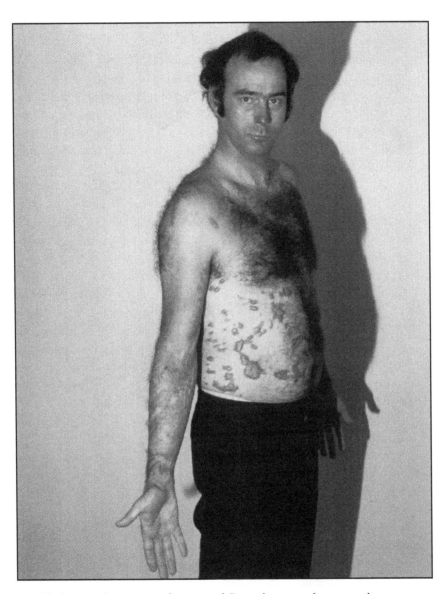

The hypotrophic scarring that covered George's torso and arms was kept somewhat in check by the use of Jobst clothing, which compresses the scars and keeps them from expanding further.

constant practice, effort, and mental awareness.

A burn survivor faces a new self. Maybe it's a self that's not as handsome as it was before, a self that physically cannot function, work, or play sports as well as before, a new person that must dress differently, deal with pain many times daily, hourly. So many adjustments. Can you see why the psychological changes can be so devastating? Professional help many times is the answer, but the true answer lies within. Find your purpose in life. Dig down deep and either accept yourself or forget it. If you can't find your reason for living, then life isn't worth living. If you can't control your mind with good thoughts, then life will continue to be an obstacle.

I thank God so often that my mental condition has always been one of stability. Now some people might question this, but the inner me is happy with myself. My background in direct selling and dealing with people paid me dividends. In fact, it helped save my life, for it's given me control over my mind.

Selling taught me that the mind is like a movie camera. If you put in bad thoughts, ugly scenes, distasteful thoughts, thoughts of hate or anger, then the image that comes out on the movie screen—which is your perception of life—also becomes bleak and depressing, just like the thoughts you put in. I learned that controlling your thinking is one of the keys to richness and achievement. Take the reverse; if you think good thoughts and take positive actions, then what you put in is what you get out. The screen that is your vision of life will be pleasant.

I had to master the art of controlling my thinking. I put good thoughts into my mind. I thought of my children, my friends, and my family. All had been so supportive. For a year I was like a lamprey eel, a sucker living off my friends and family. They fed me faith, strength, and encouragement. They constantly reiterated their love and feelings for me. I learned that love was probably the most important four-letter word in the English language. I learned that saying "I love you" to friends and family is nothing to be ashamed of. How many people go through life questioning whether a certain person loves them or not? Why play games? Be up front with people. Be open about your feelings.

But enough with the psychology! Back to my real-life situation!

27

Our business continued to flounder. Our construction losses were up to $60,000 and counting. Christmas was not far away, and I knew our slowest season was not going to help our business. December through March is the slowest time of the year for recreational real estate. Salary and overhead is a 12-month commitment, of course, so our expenses didn't stop during this period.

Our business could not go forward until our unsuccessful building experience was put to rest. We thought our financial woes had ended. We started a new project in Falmouth on Cape Cod. We figured we would let the judicial system solve our woes with Bruce, the thieving contractor. But lawsuits are a long-term process. Bruce continued to be vengeful to us for firing him.

We figured moving to a new area and starting fresh would be helpful. We were wrong again. We moved a business trailer into our Falmouth property as a temporary sales office. The third night the trailer was on site, we got another disturbing phone call. Our trailer had burned to the ground.

There was too much coincidence to our problems. The district attorney put out an all points bulletin for Bruce. The fire marshal introduced us to the hard realities of getting a arson conviction. "There is less than a two percent conviction rate," he said. "If you catch your villain with the match in his hand," he added, "there's still a chance he will go free."

We now knew that Bruce was a pathological liar who could most likely pass a lie detector test. Four months later, he did exactly that. Discouraged but not defeated, we held out hope that while we couldn't get him for arson, we would still be able to win our lawsuit regarding the fraud he had perpetrated on us.

Unfortunately, that was not to be. Bruce soon skipped town and disappeared out of our reach and out of our lives once and for all. Certainly, living every day with the knowledge that Bruce was running around in our neck of the woods, fully capable of using fire against me again, was unsettling at best and terrifying at worst. So, in some ways, knowing he had cleared out for other parts of the country was a relief.

As Christmas approached, thoughts of being away from Anne and the children were crushing. I went about my way buying the kids presents, just as if nothing had really happened.

We decided that for the kids' sake, I would come to the house Christmas Eve, help wrap the gifts and spend the night in the guest room. It was always hard to face the fact of being a guest in my home, but so goes life.

On Christmas Eve, Joanne and I attended a party at her brother's house. With our friendship now a relationship, I was becoming scared. I needed her so much, but I wasn't ready emotionally. She was so good for me, so understanding of my needs physically and emotionally, always giving and receiving so little in return. I was needy, and I drew from the relationship what I needed to survive.

I decided to leave the party early around 10:00 P.M. Most women would have told me to go to hell, but Joanne seemed so understanding of the situation. Her true love for me put her needs second.

I arrived in Westford at 11:15, planning maybe a cocktail and a quiet wrapping of presents. As I walked in I found that Anne was passed out on the couch. Steve and David were still up running around. I was bullshit, but I figured that when you're in the process of divorce, you give up certain rights to judge other people.

The kids were my main concern. I hugged them and shuffled them up to bed. We casually said prayers as we always did. The conversation quickly turned to Santa Claus. They were so excited. Ages 4 and 5! What a truly great age for kids and Christmas. Thank God Santa was coming because they were both anxious to go to sleep. I thought I hid my feeling of anger over Anne's condition well.

Now the presents and Anne lay ahead. After about four shakes Anne finally rose to her feet. She explained that she had been at an office Christmas party with the kids, one mile up the road at Frank's Citgo. I didn't mind the party so much, but was this a place for two kids? The Christmas spirit forced me to hold back my angry thoughts and words. After all, Anne was still embroiled in a tremendous guilt-complex herself. Divorced life for her was different. She was struggling to find herself, her life, her purpose. She still carried the guilt of our marriage breaking up at such an untimely period. She still could not figure out why she didn't love me. She was working now, maintaining the house, and trying to be a good mother. To say the least, she had her hands full emotionally.

Around 1 in the morning we finished wrapping presents and assembling bicycles, toys and garages, all with the 20 pages of simple instructions. As usual, I had extra bolts and nuts left over.

I decided to bring in Anne's present. This was a hard gift to buy, but I couldn't see going through the day without a gift, a reminder that I still cared.

I figured I would buy a safe gift. We had lost so many personal items in the fire that many walls were still bare. I remembered that Anne's favorite artist was Carolyn Blish. I bought a nice picture of a beach scene. It would fit nicely in the living room over the couch. I had scouted the location weeks earlier.

I carried in the big package. I wanted to put it under the tree, but I sensed that Anne wanted to open it now, so I said, "Okay, if you want."

Quick as a child, she removed the wrapping. Excitement filled her eyes.

"Georgie, a Blish, my favorite! You didn't have to."

"I couldn't help it."

Suddenly Anne's joy turned to tears. She held me and sobbed. I couldn't understand why. I would get my answer in a few hours.

28

I managed to get a few hours sleep in the guest room. Christmas morning was announced at 6:00 by the shrieking sound of two excited kids.

"Dad! Dad! Santa came!"

Part of their excitement for sure was having Dad home for Christmas. We quickly raced to the living room. The procedure for the last five years had been for me to systematically hand out the presents one by one. If I didn't do this, then Christmas would last ten minutes with these excited kids.

Little by little, Steve and Dave opened their gifts. "Dad! Mom! Look, the Incredible Hulk, a bike, coloring books, Sesame Street Garage, Etch-A-Sketch" and on and on. So many presents. Were they learning the true meaning of Christmas, I wondered.

Halfway through the presents, much like a kid, I found myself looking for a present, a card, something addressed to Dad, to George from Anne, or to Dad from Santa. Just something to know I was thought of, appreciated, and loved. As the pile of unopened presents dwindled, the knot in my stomach became larger and tighter.

Was there a present, a card, anything for Dad? Had Santa forgotten me this year? Maybe I was a bad boy. I tried to stay excited right till the last present. I hid my hurt well. Not a present, nothing for Dad. Is this what I deserved? Was Anne so preoccupied with herself that she couldn't or wouldn't at least get a card? I couldn't believe it or understand it.

My hurt deepened. As Anne prepared my breakfast, David asked, "Why didn't Santa bring you something, Dad?"

"He did, Dave. He brought me you and Steve."

I had to run to the upstairs bathroom. I tried to hold back the tears, but they wouldn't stop.

I wanted so much for someone to hold me, to tell me it was okay, to love me, to understand my feelings. I struggled for composure. Oh, well, I will go to my parents for dinner and presents. I guess that's where the real Christmas would be. I knew for sure they loved me.

My insides were still churning. Anne had an afternoon lunch date. Her family had not even invited her anywhere. They rarely ever got together for family gatherings. I wanted to say something to Anne, but I couldn't. I decided to leave her a note. I had to tell her how I felt. Somehow in the bathroom I found time to compose this note:

Dear Anne,

I found it hard to accept this Christmas. It's so hard for me and I'm sure it's hard for you. You have insisted to me that you want to remain friends, remain close for the kids' sake. I'm so hurt right now that words can't express it. I can't understand or accept why you couldn't have even given me a card, or a small token from the kids. I'm sorry to say, Anne, that if I mean that little to you, or if you don't care anymore, then fine, forget me. You've probably lost the best friend you have ever had. Good-bye.

George

I headed for my parents' home for a big turkey dinner, taking the boys with me. The kids were ecstatic. Another Christmas, more presents, more fun.

It was hard facing the family on this happy holiday without Anne at my side. For eight straight years we had come as a family, but from now on it would be different. My dreams of a happy family had disintegrated.

The worst moment came when my sister Elaine asked in front of everyone, "What did Anne get you for Christmas?"

I couldn't tell the truth. They would be too judgmental. Somehow I always managed to spare Anne in any conversation. I never once badmouthed her. It wasn't right. Besides, no one had all the facts to be judgmental anyway.

"Oh, a few pieces of clothing," I said and quickly changed the conversation.

Soon it was time to pack up the kids, take them home, and then head back to Weymouth. We neatly packed the many Christmas presents into boxes and bags. We paid our respects and said goodbye. The kids quickly fell asleep in the car. Steve and Dave always argued over who would sit next to me on the way home. They wanted to be next to me, to be reassured of my love for them. They looked so peaceful asleep.

Christmas had been a long, tiring and mentally exhaustive day. We arrived back in Westford. It was time to pick up a babysitter for the boys since Anne wasn't scheduled to be home yet. As I drove in the driveway, I was surprised to see her car in the driveway. As we walked into the family room Anne was stretched out on the couch. I could tell by the distant, gaunt look on her face that she was upset.

As I moved closer I could see she had roadmap-like lines in her eyes. No doubt she had been crying for some time. Anne came to embrace me, to say once again that she was sorry. Somehow I couldn't accept her apology this time. I had heard "I'm sorry" so many times from Anne that the words began to lose their meaning.

Anne struggled for words. "I'm just emotionally drained this year. I didn't send Christmas cards to anyone. I couldn't get into the spirit. There has been so much on my mind. I want you to be my friend. Your friendship is important to me. Please don't stop being my friend."

I didn't buy her explanation. I was trying to understand but couldn't.

I said, "I have to get going; it's a long ride to Weymouth."

I kissed the kids goodbye, turned, and once again walked out of their lives.

The 60-mile ride from Westford to Weymouth many times was quite relaxing and therapeutic for me. It gave me time for peace and quiet, with no phones ringing and no interruptions. Many times I arrived home and couldn't even remember one mile of roadway. It always amazed me how my eyes could physically follow the road and safely return me home, but subconsciously my mind could be miles away. My subconscious mind could totally escape the physical me.

I couldn't wait to get back to Weymouth. I knew Joanne would be anxiously awaiting my return. I always felt comfortable in her arms. But as our feelings grew for one another, it became difficult to involve her in any discussion involving Anne, because Joanne had appraised the facts as she knew them and had made a judgment about Anne.

Many times she would say, "I don't care how mixed up Anne is emotionally. I would never abandon my husband, especially at a time of crisis when you needed me the most. How could she?"

Joanne in every way was performing the tasks of a wife. She watched out for my best interests and she made sure I didn't overdo it physically, that I did my exercises, and that I got enough sleep.

At times our relationship seemed so stable, but so many times I found myself running. I was unwilling to let go emotionally with her. I held back from telling her I loved her because, for me, saying those words meant a commitment, a commitment I just couldn't make at this time.

Many times I struggled with my own definition of love. How much should I give? When and how should I give it? Had I failed at a marriage and love when I felt I had given so much? Why didn't it work? If I played by the same rules would that mean that my relationship with Joanne would end up in disaster and hurt? I didn't want to face these questions now. I needed time to get my life in order. The physical me and mental me were not sufficiently healed.

So many times I felt guilty about my relationship with Joanne. Joanne was giving so much and receiving very little in return. The percentages were definitely lopsided.

The little love, little stroking, little attention that Joanne needed at times became such a big effort for me. It was not that I didn't care. My brain felt like a big beach ball that had all the air squeezed out. Many times I just stumbled along not thinking out my actions, and, yes, many times I unknowingly hurt her.

At times I struggled to explain my feelings. "Jo, at times I feel like a new car on the freeway. Cruising along with you feels so good, so safe, so comfortable, but many times I come to forks in the road, detours, or exits that lead me astray. They lead me to drinking, raising hell, and other women. Why, I don't know. I suppose many times it was a way of releasing my anger."

Releasing my anger was important, but many times my releases became Joanne's hurt. I knew deep down inside that she understood. Joanne, too, had been through divorce and for a time had also raised hell. It's a cleansing process.

29

I learned that there is a correlation between a happy home life and any sales effort. Selling for a commission is not like a nine-to-five job. I couldn't sit at a desk, fake my way through the day and collect my paycheck on Friday. Selling is such a mental business. You have to be up all the time, optimistic, excitable like a child, and, of course, positive minded. This was all hard to achieve given what I was going through.

When the cancer of a failing relationship hits, most times it takes a mental toll. The days that I felt down were a direct result of the problems I faced because of the fire and divorce. When I finally understood this, I set out as I always had and started to control my thinking. I would control the thoughts that I fed into my brain. When in a selling situation, I began acting as I had always actually felt in the past: razor sharp, right to the point with as much facts, knowledge and enthusiasm as I could muster. Selling is much like a triple play in baseball, the execution has to be flawless. Finally, by acting like my old self, I became my old self and put my winning sales style back in place.

For 10 hours a day I ate, slept and drank real estate. It was time to execute, a time to stop feeling sorry for myself. I had a financial commitment beyond most people's imagination. The divorce was costing me $400 per week. That was one hell of a nut.

But I no longer worried about the problem. I worked on the solution. A key to success is spending most of your time in life working on solutions to problems, not dwelling on the problem. After all, you know the problem. Why keep beating it to death? I realized the problem was me. The solution was to regain my winning sales style. That's the solution to the problem.

Things and problems in life won't change unless you do. .For things to change, you have to change; you have to get better. So many times in life I hear people talking about how broke they are, how they can't do this, they can't do that. It's the fault of inflation, it's the fault of the economy, it's the fault of the weather!

That's a loser talking. Why not take a night course, a part-time job, work harder at your own job? Why not do something to solve the problem? Solutions come about because of actions, not talk. Actions do speak louder than words. I always wanted to be a winner. I learned through my rebirth that winners never quit and quitters never win.

Six months after physically returning to work I walked into my partner's office and said, "Dick, I'm back."

He naturally looked puzzled since I'd been showing up at work for months.

"I've just been going through the motions," I said. "I've been healing, but now I'm ready mentally!"

Dealing with divorce was becoming easier, too, or so I thought. Anne was now dating Ken; he was the Westford neighbor she had mentioned going to the movies with a few times while I was hospitalized. I knew of him, but had never met him. I met him unexpectedly on a Saturday morning, a day that by coincidence happened to be the first anniversary of my accident. As I drove in the driveway that morning with a box of donuts at around 9:30, there was a car in the yard. I wondered who was at the house this early on a Saturday.

As I entered the house Anne said, "George, I would like you to meet Ken."

"Hi, George," Ken said as he put his hand out to shake mine.

One of the many adjustments of divorce is to eventually see your former spouse with another man or woman. The thought of another man touching my wife, sleeping with her, hugging my kids, giving them orders...it hurt.

This reality of divorce quickly hit me that morning and it set me back. I was depressed all day. I tried to get in tune with my feelings. I now faced another new and difficult situation to cope with, just one of dozens that had been thrown at me in the past 12 months. Thank God I was blessed with a positive attitude and a sense of humor. I found it much easier to laugh than to cry.

Fortunately, the next day was Sunday, and Sunday mornings always excited me. After nine years of traveling to and from Martha's Vineyard selling real estate, I still got excited. I often wondered why this was true. Selling was the only profession I knew of that could change your lifestyle in a short period of time.

Selling intrigued me on two levels. The first level was a financial one. The law of averages in selling was a law I loved. The law basically says that if you show your product or service to large numbers of people, some will buy, some will say I'm not interested, some will say I can't afford it, and some will lie or mislead you, but over time, you'll be able to identify your sales success average. When I finally understood this I never got upset about the people who said no to what I was selling, because I knew I was that much closer to a yes.

I always correlated this sales success average with baseball. If a batter in baseball had a .300 career average, it meant that every ten times he came to the plate he got three hits, and the other seven times he was an out, a statistic, a loser. This intrigued me because a .300 career hitter is considered great.

I also knew that great baseball hitters practiced a lot, worked hard, and strove to improve their percentages. I worked the same in my profession. I kept a record of the number of people I showed real estate to. After eight years I had brought roughly 1,000 prospects to Martha's Vineyard. Out of the 1,000 I had 450 sales or a .450 batting average. I had noticed that my average was improving. My first few years I averaged .230 and then .300, and slowly .350 and now .500 and .600. I was definitely getting better each year. I now knew that if I had 10 prospects on a Sunday, the odds were good I would make a sale to five of them. Incredible!

I also knew that to get 10 people to look at the property I had to talk to 20 people, which meant talking to four or five people each day, Monday through Friday. Out of 20 phone calls, 10 would look and five would buy. What a great formula. I now knew that my financial income was directly proportionate to the number of people I showed property to. This may seem so basic, but most sales people never understand this concept.

The next level that intrigued me about selling was what I called the Love Me Principle. This is very simple in theory. Basically at the end of the sale, I wanted all of my prospects to love me. In theory this is simple, but putting it in practice is most difficult.

To leverage the "Love Me" principle, I had to exert professionalism from start to finish. I had to show excitement and enthusiasm about my product. Excitement is contagious. Most people are not around excitable people all that often. So many people remarked to me, "Gee, you're really excited about real estate." The truth of the matter was yes, I was!

I painted a picture. I showed people how real estate could help their future, could be a vehicle to get them somewhere—retirement, a savings plan, an education for the children, a tax hedge. I found out what their goals in life were, what made them tick. If I found their "hot button," I could show them a way to achieve their goal.

People in general can learn to love you by talking about "feeling things."

Not questions about the bad weather, the long car ride from Boston, work on Monday morning, or other potentially negative things. Negative feelings produce negative results.

Instead, I constantly talked about positive feeling things. "Did you know that land values have appreciated from $7,000 a lot to $19,000 a lot in five years?" "How will you pay for the children's education?" "I'm glad you took time out of your busy schedule to look at an opportunity." "There's a limited supply of land on this island; someday it will be gone."

I tried to make people laugh, relax, have fun, and enjoy my company. It was a simple expectation but it was amazing how little people laugh and enjoy themselves. It is such a challenge to meet an unknown person, spend a few hours and feel like you've know him all your life. This is what I called the "warming up" process. It was much easier to sell to your friends versus selling to "cold people" or strangers.

Many sales people lack perseverance. If they don't make a sale or a commission within a short period of time, they lose interest and move on to supposedly better vistas. I learned not to quit easily. I believe a winner *never* quits and a quitter *never* wins.

I truly believe my knowledge of selling helped keep me alive in the hospital. I never thought of dying. I never thought of giving up. I can remember lying in bed saying to myself, "Well, here I am. I can't do anything about work. I can't worry about things I can't affect, only those things I can affect."

My immediate goal became survival. I funneled all my energies into positiveness, persistence, and excellence at doing the things that would expedite my healing. I gave my body 120 percent of what it asked for and it responded. People were amazed at how fast I healed. It wasn't so miraculous when you realize I was one of the few patients to force feed 10,000 calories a day. That's what the doctor ordered. Doctors don't want to hear how hard the task is. Sure it was hard. Do you have any choice when your life is at stake? It didn't take me long to answer that question.

30

One year after you've been burned is a milestone. The one-year period is most significant with regard to scarring since it takes from six months to one year for scar tissue to form. The ugly striations slowly form and push their way over healing areas. Scars seem to particularly like joints. The tissue slowly creeps to the edge of the joint and then with one quick jump it straddles the joint forming a web-like effect. As the scars mature the tissue gets very stiff and forms rock hard cord striations.

Scar tissue has very little elasticity so the joint areas particularly feel the impact because you're constantly bending your fingers, knees and forearms. Even by continually exercising, burn survivors many times lose the battle to scarring. I worked very hard at doing 50 pushups and 50 sit-ups each day. Some days exercising seemed relatively easy; other days the scars seemed like steel cables that didn't want to pull or stretch. I could now straighten both arms, but the cord-like scar tissue was quite heavy on my left arm. After a year, I stopped wearing my elastic Jobst arm sleeves. They had done a tremendous job in flattening the scars on my arms; cosmetically, the scars looked better.

My ribs continued to be sore and stiff. The uncovered scar tissue had raised havoc on my chest. Reddish purple bumps of scar tissue were now well formed. The pockets in many areas looked like moon craters—smooth tissue, then massive canyons, then open plains. Bumpy roads still made me wince because ribs act like shock absorbers for the upper torso.

Both legs from the knees down were improving. The purple-colored grafts were now turning bright red; the colors I never thought would fade were now lightening. I used to have to shift from foot to foot because the tingling sensations were too tough to bear, but now I could stand still because the circulation was improving.

Not a day went by without my thanking God for a second chance. I never questioned Him as to why this had happened to me as I heard from so many people. I never believed that God sits in heaven on a big chair pointing His finger saying, "Okay, it's time to give George a hard time; it's time for him to suffer." God gives us the gift of life. It's up to us to do what we want.

Life is much like a train ride. We all leave the station at birth, heading in the same direction, some get off or die at the first station, and some get off and die at the last station, but we all have to get off eventually. When the doctor gave me a one in five chance to survive, I was hanging off the edge of the train. I almost let go, but somehow I held on. I kept clinging to the railing, hoping I would make the next stop. Each day I got stronger. I wouldn't let go. I wanted to live.

Summer turned quickly to fall. I couldn't stay in the bright sunshine. There weren't many beach days or sunbathing days, just brief five- to 10-minute intervals in the sun. My thin healing skin was still very susceptible to the sun's powerful ultraviolet rays. I always wore my baseball cap to keep the rays off my face.

The kids and I had some great baseball scrimmages. They were growing so fast. We practiced for hours. I wanted them to inherit the competitiveness that my father had taught me. Play hard, give it your best, play to win, and be a good sport. I felt these philosophies in sports overflowed into my personal and business life and were often beneficial.

One day Stephen lined a drive over my head and my immediate reaction was to leap high to catch it as I always had in the past. I jumped with full arm extension over my head and instantly felt excruciating pain. I dropped to my knees, holding my left side, fighting to hold back tears. That damn scar tissue just wouldn't stretch, only tear.

I quickly felt two sets of gentle hands on my shoulder. The boys' loving, caring, concerned eyes peered at me.

"Are you okay, Dad? Did you hurt yourself? Are you okay? What happened, Dad?"

"My ribs still hurt, boys," I said gingerly. "I'm okay."

"Do you want to take a break, Dad?"

The boys had become very protective of me. We embraced, and they both said they loved me and the pain gradually went away.

I was pleased with the relationship I had developed with Stephen and Dave. They were learning the days of the week in school and they knew that every Wednesday and Saturday I would be there. I knew I had to see them as much as possible. The values of life that I cherished had to be taught on a part-time basis. I always encouraged conversation—with caring, sharing, feeling, loving, expressing, and openness. I wanted the boys to know that I was their friend and would always be there. I tried consciously not to have a casual relationship with my children as I have seen so many divorced dads do. Casual feelings result in casualties.

From the start I wanted our divorce to be different and it certainly was. Anne and I had made a motto not to alienate the children. So many divorced parents pit the children against the opposite parent. If they only knew the danger, harm, and stupidity of this they never would do it. Anne and I tried to maintain a friendship, one that was still a caring relationship without passionate, marital love. Although we were divorced, the children felt secure around us.

Anne and I often went to supper to discuss our personal lives, finances, romances and most of all the children, schoolwork, discipline and so on. Many people asked me, "How can you even talk to her after what she did to you?" But I never felt Anne really did anything to me, at least not intentionally. If anything, I admired her honesty. She didn't love me and she made a decision and told me. I'll always respect her for that. So many people waste their lives in unhappy marriages. Everyone pays the price. We all have a right to be happy. Staying married meant unhappiness for Anne. Slowly but surely, I was realizing that divorce was best for us.

The time I was spending with Joanne for the most part was quality time. I realized that in my marriage I had lacked good, positive, supportive love and stroking. I was coming out of my shell. I was finding the real me.

Acceptance seems like such a simple word, but to me it was an important one. Joanne totally accepted me for me. I didn't have to change my ways for her. She was teaching me more about love than I cared to let her know. It scared me because it felt good. I struggled not to let her know how I felt. I was reassessing all my values and definitions of love.

I often wondered where I went astray in my marriage, but other than maybe working too hard, I couldn't think of any major mistake I had made. I had struggled through college, got married, lived in a three-decker house, had two small children, a 1961 Ford convertible and no money in the bank. To say the least we were unhappy, struggling, and going nowhere. So I decided to leave the accounting world and entered an uncertain real estate field.

For three years there were disappointments, many more no's than yesses as my law of averages wasn't working well yet, but within four years I developed a style. We had taken a two-week winter Caribbean vacation for four straight years. We had the nice home in the suburbs, new cars, money in the bank, and two healthy kids. But for some reason, Anne didn't love me. I couldn't understand why and to this day I don't understand why. But

I saw no reason to punish her by not maintaining a cordial relationship, especially when it benefited the kids so much.

As Joanne was helping me understand, the ways of the heart are mysterious and just because I couldn't understand why Anne didn't love me didn't mean I should shove her totally out of my life. All that would achieve would be to hurt our sons, the most important thing we shared from our marriage.

31

The fall of 1980 turned out to be the biggest selling season ever for our company. I was selling in an economy with double-digit interest rates and inflation. Everyone else was complaining about the problem and not thinking of a solution. For a solid 90 days I sold deal after deal. After every purchase and sale agreement and every deposit, I got more and more excited. My enthusiasm was contagious. I inspired so many people. Their words of praise to me for what I was doing in spite of the odds inspired me to do even more.

My father always said, "Do the best at whatever you do in life." I was living this out. In 90 days I personally sold 50 lots and 10 homes. For most brokers, this was two years of work squeezed into 90 days. By earning big dollars my financial problems soon disappeared, and that $400 check to Anne at times was easy to write.

As I benefited personally, so did the business. The unpaid bills file in our accountant's desk quickly started to shrink, and those distressing phone calls from venders hounding us for money also disappeared.

And, yes, a positive outlook on business started to pay dividends on my mental attitude. The trips to Westford to visit seemed to go better. The quality of time spent with the boys was better. Even the kids recognized that their "old Dad" was back, with all the love and enthusiasm that they had once remembered.

As my strength grew and I took on more activities, I needed to learn to work smart and budget my time wisely. Joanne took time, the children took two days a week, friends and relatives took time, work took time. My precious time was being demanded by so many people who wanted to be with me.

Every Tuesday afternoon I went to Peter Bent Brigham Hospital to meet one-on-one with burn patients. After these sessions I participated in a weekly Burn Support Group attended by a psychiatrist, a burn technician, a Social Services director, and three to five burn survivors. These meetings and related activities soon became an important part of my life.

I felt comfortable going to the first meeting because Maureen, whom I had met while in the hospital, would be there. We had continued communication for several months. Maureen and I were lucky; our scars could be well concealed with proper clothing. But soon a man named John came to the meeting who had incurred tremendous facial disfigurement. I had never met anyone like this before. When I first met John I couldn't look at his face, not because it upset me but because I just felt so much compassion and sorrow for him. My God, here was someone far worse off than me. At least I looked okay in a suit.

An amazing revelation occurred to me. After I listened to John talk for a while, I found myself listening to what he had to say and not noticing what he looked like. I was reaching beyond his scars. Most people who meet facially disfigured victims are repulsed. They don't know what caused the scars. They've never seen scars like this, so they don't know if "it" might be contagious. Most facially disfigured people get reactions from the public that are difficult to cope with. Facially disfigured burn survivors should assure the new people they meet by saying, "It's okay; I was burned." Most of the time this helps set people at ease.

The meetings of the burn group were very therapeutic. I decided I wanted to meet more burn survivors, to help in any way I could. All burn survivors have a common bond. We can all relate to the pain, suffering, long hospitalizations, surgical procedures, psychological problems, and the whole gamut of problems we have encountered.

I began to question why weren't there other burn groups. Why was there no national organization for victims to turn to?

I felt the medical community was failing to recognize a major problem that was being caused by the new improved burn care. As little as ten years ago before my accident, I almost certainly would have died. At that time, people who suffered major burns commonly died from infection, pneumonia, or renal failure. But advances in sterile procedures, grafting, ointments, creams and overall technology were keeping patients alive. Each year hundreds of survivors of major burns were now returning to society; most of these individuals faced mammoth physical and psychological challenges with little support from the medical community.

I couldn't understand why the medical community did not recognize this. The news always covered the fire stories by saying so many people perished in such and such a fire. What about the ones who survived? How are they doing? Most people don't know or care because many major burn victims become recluses or turn to alcohol or drugs to relieve their psychological pain.

One of my goals quickly became to educate the public about the problems the growing population of burn survivors face. Our burn group continued to grow. We printed a Discharge Booklet because we found most hospitals had very little literature for patients to read when they went home. There were so many needs.

One day someone mentioned an organization called The Phoenix Society to me. I did some research and found that this group for burn survivors was located in Pennsylvania. I sent off a letter, not knowing what to expect in return.

Shortly thereafter I received a letter from Alan Jeffrey Breslau. He sent me a pamphlet that explained that the phoenix is a legendary bird that was reborn from the ashes of a fire; it was the symbol of rebirth, something burn survivors know about. The brochure further explained that the society was a self-help group for burn survivors and family members. I didn't at this point understand how family members were victims of fire. The brochure also showed the badly burned face and hands of what the brochure said was a man. Mr. Beslau's letter never mentioned that these were photographs of him.

Immediately I felt our informal weekly group meeting could benefit by a national affiliation. I sent a letter to Alan inviting him to Boston. He responded by saying that he was coming to Boston in the near future. We arranged a meeting.

I soon learned Alan had written a book called *At the Time of My Death.* It was a factual account of his struggle to survive after a fiery plane crash in upstate New York. His upper torso was burned to the bone in many places. He struggled and survived through over 50 operations. After reading the book, I was even more anxious to meet this survivor who had so much to say.

When I first met Alan, my reaction was much the same as my experience in meeting John. I felt immediate compassion, sorrow, and empathy. There was so much scarring, missing fingers, a dysfunctional eye, a wig, sunglasses, plastic ears, and on and on. This man had been literally rebuilt. Somehow he had survived.

As had happened with John, once Alan started to talk I found myself looking beyond his scars and listening. He was telling us how he coped.

"You know, when a beautiful woman meets a man she gets a reaction," he said. "It's up to her to do what she wants to do with the reaction. She can be friendly and strike up a conversation or she can turn and walk away. It's her choice. I also get a reaction when I meet people, but I'm the opposite of the pretty woman. I'm ugly; I'm scarred; I'm repulsive. But guess what? I also get a reaction from people. It's up to me to decide what to do. I can ignore it and walk away, or I can say 'It's okay, I was burned; don't be afraid.' Almost immediately the unknown person shows relief. Listen to what people have to say, look beyond looks. Listen to words. It's one of the keys in life that people miss out on. They point fingers, they stare, they ridicule, they pull their children away. They react with unkind words because they don't understand. Give burn survivors a chance, a chance to return to society as normal persons. We are normal; we are only scarred."

Alan talked about coping, which is one of the biggest obstacles a burn survivor faces. He explained his way of coping and accepting his condition as "life." His positive attitude reminded me so much of myself.

We also viewed a film of a child whose face had been badly burned. A gas pilot light in a heater had ignited some gasoline vapors from an open can of gas. I now began to understand causes of accidents. Most fires are needless. The public is in the first grade of the learning process for fire prevention. Most people think it's never going to be them. Alan also spoke of legislation he was involved in to help prevent fires and burns. He opened up a whole new field of curiosity for me.

As a young therapy group we always seemed concerned about the size of our group. We weren't growing. Alan pointed out that a group can be one person helping one person. The main purpose of The Phoenix Society is to help people, he said. If you help one person, you may have saved a life.

Our emphasis in our group now turned to truly helping people help other people. I started to deeply question issues I had glossed over. I began to think about my accident. Gee, a pilot light had caused my accident, and a pilot light ignited combustible vapors from Maureen's camping fluid. I read of a pilot light in a hot water heater hidden in a bathroom linen closet igniting gasoline fumes as a mother scrubbed tar off her two children. All these stories horrified me. We all had forgotten about pilot lights.

I already had met at least ten people who had been burned by using a flammable solution near a gas stove. It must be foreseeable. I began to analyze the question of whether these accidents could have been prevented. I started to look into appliances. I found out that most appliances carry warning labels that say "Warning: do not use flammable solutions in the area." I wondered why gas stoves didn't have a warning label to remind people that the pilot light is continuously burning.

I kept hearing of pilot-light related accidents. Even though I was negligent in using gasoline, the question became "Does the manufacturer have any duty to warn the public of any inherent dangers in using their appliance?" I felt they most certainly did.

I contacted a law firm. Why wasn't there a warning label on a stove? It certainly could not be a cost factor to stick on a little label. So why weren't they doing it? Could it possibly be that this little two-cent label might hurt sales? Maybe consumers would buy electric stoves if they saw a warning. Our research intensified. Why couldn't we find one law case where an individual sued a stove manufacturer for its failure to warn the public about the pilot light? Could all these manufacturers be settling out of court? Could they have made a conscious decision not to warn for competitive reasons? I concluded this was the case.

(Note: After the time period covered in this book, I sued both the manufacturer of the stove and eventually the manufacturer of the gas can, which also lacked a warning label telling consumers not to use the can near a pilot light. I could write another whole book on the unbelievable twists and turns this litigation took over what eventually was a 13-year period. But the end result was that after winning a $10 million judgment against the gas can company, the case was thrown out of court because we hadn't added the gas can company to the lawsuit until after the three-year statute of limitations had expired.

Why hadn't we added the gas can company to the suit until too late? Originally, I could not remember who the manufacturer of the can was and since we believed the can was destroyed in the fire, we thought this was a dead end. But it turned out that the original attorney who had been put on my case was a neophyte who had never asked for the original police file! This file included a role of undeveloped film taken in my kitchen after the fire; once developed, the photos clearly showed a portion of the gas can that hadn't burned and the manufacturer's name was easily readable.

When my original attorney left the law firm, the new, more experienced lawyer who took over my case immediately found this evidence. He was horrified that the first lawyer hadn't found it. The evidence helped us to win the case against the gas can company. However, on appeal, the gas can company managed to get the verdict thrown out because of the statute of limitations problem. How maddening to think that the needed evidence had been lying in the police file from day one!

My only recourse at that point was to bring a malpractice suit against the law firm and the original lawyer who had made the error that led to the statue of limitations problem. So the upshot was that I became the first person in the history of Massachusetts courts to win a malpractice suit against a law firm that had actually won—and then lost due to what many would call legal technicalities—a multi-million dollar court case for him. The senior partner of the law firm felt so badly about how things had turned out that he told me he would do everything in his power to have the malpractice case settled in my favor. That eventually did happen and we settled the malpractice case for $1.5 million, 40 percent of which, of course, went to my new attorney. Certainly a much smaller payday than $10 million!

I'm happy to report, though, that after all the dust settled, the gas can company did change its labeling so its products specifically warn people to keep the can away from pilot lights, gas heaters, and similar appliances.

32

Little by little, our burn group was getting recognition. Calls came in from social workers and rehab specialists asking for help for burn patients. A burn patient who was at a crossroads in his life called; he had many unanswered questions. Each time I spoke to someone, I felt good about what I was doing. The therapy always wasn't immediately noticeable, but it did help. Seeing me up and around, working, living a normal life, surviving helped inspire many burn survivors.

I now began to understand more about how spouses, children, parents, siblings, other relatives, and friends suffer when someone they love becomes a burn survivor.

What about my own children? They envisioned their dad running out of the house fully engulfed with flames. They saw life and death flash before their eyes. After the fire, they saw my ugly swelling and scarring each week. They lost all of their childhood toys and personal belongings. What effect would this have on their lives and their attitudes about life?

How about my now ex-wife, Anne? In seconds on a Saturday afternoon her husband was tragically burned, her house and personal belongings were totally destroyed, and her children cried out for help. She temporarily moved into a thoughtful neighbor's house, visited her husband faithfully each day, praying and hoping that he would live. She dealt with, "What will I do if George dies? What will the boys and I live on? What will his scars look like? Will I still love him? If I divorce George now, will everyone judge me?" So many huge questions to face in such a short period of time.

Because our marriage was already in trouble, the timing of the fire could not have been worse. Anne had so much guilt to deal with. But while I was hospitalized, she dug down deep and put on her suit of armor. She never once cried in front of me. She showed me so much love and strength. Despite her inner problems, fears, and doubts about our marriage, she went the extra mile to give me the love and hope I truly needed to survive. She taught me so much about commitment. She knew that I could die anytime from day one to day 42. She faced my possible death every day and dealt with it.

Friends and relatives were also tested. Countless friends called the hospital only to hear, "He's critical, no visitors." They also carried the worry and fear of my death. Not being able to visit, so many people felt so helpless. I later heard countless stories of my friends becoming despondent or angry. I saw the worried faces as they approached my hospital bedroom door once they were allowed to visit. They feared what they might now see.

Life works in such mysterious ways. Your faith and belief in God are seriously tested when you face death. As you lie in bed in danger of dying, you tend to review your life. I recall reviewing the good points I had accomplished. I also thought of my faults. I spoke to God and told him that if I survived, I would be a better person. I would strive to do more and become better. I would find my reason for living.

Mom and Dad were always noted for their belief and faithfulness to God and their religion. They both constantly prayed for and hoped for a miracle. My mother prayed that my face would heal, free from ugly scars. They went to faith healing sessions at Mission Hill Church in Roxbury, a short walk from the hospital.

They attended this service one evening when I had developed an infection. Fever had set in, and they knew this infection could kill me. As the Father McDonough, the priest, passed my mother he splashed her with holy water. A feeling of grace overcame her, and she passed out for 10 minutes. When she came to, Father McDonough told her I would survive. The next morning Dr. O'Connor told my mother that my fever had disappeared and my infection was under control.

Learning of these experiences inspired me to greater heights. The true value of The Phoenix Society as a self-help group for burn survivors *and* family members became clearer to me every day, and, as the months passed, I became more involved with this wonderful organization. For me, this was turning into a crusade. The "burned world" was crying out for help. I could see the merits of this self-help group. I came to realize how needless most fires were. I felt possessed to tell the world about our group, to help prevent fires, and to educate the public about fire prevention and about the needs of burn survivors.

My friend Maureen Moriarity was appointed Assistant Area Coordinator for the Society. We worked well together. Every Tuesday we headed for Boston, visiting patients from all walks of life. We often commented on the bond all burn survivors have. Anyone who survives the catacombs of hell has a bond. The phoenix, which in Egyptian mythology consumed itself in fire only to be reborn, was taking on more meaning for us.

Case after case, hospital after hospital, week after week, the stories were so different, but so similar. We heard about so much needless suffering caused by so many needless fires:

"I was making a cup of coffee, but my bathrobe caught on fire."

"I threw a log in a wood-burning stove and my bathrobe caught fire."

"My child tripped over the portable heater."

"I forgot about the pilot light on the stove."

"I fell asleep with a cigarette in my hand."

"My gasoline tank exploded in a rear end collision."

I started an assault to convince the news media they should put some effort into educating the public on fire prevention. Door after door was shut in my face. I heard, "It's a good cause, but our station doesn't have any public service announcement time left." Or a polite but noncommittal, "We'll consider it." I knew my law of averages had to work here too and that after so many rejections, I must be getting closer to a yes.

Finally came a ray of hope. A newsman for WBZ-TV in Boston named Charles Austin seemed to understand my pleas. He was courteous, compassionate and, most of all, understanding. After nine months of trying to get the story on the air, Charles finally called me on November 24, 1980.

"We're going to give your burn group a one minute plug on the 11:00 P.M. news tomorrow," he said. "Call the station tomorrow afternoon and talk to Beth O'Connell. You know Beth?" I couldn't remember her, and acknowledged that I didn't recall meeting her.

That night I threw together two pans of homemade lasagna. The burn group was coming to my apartment the next day for a Thanksgiving dinner and so was Channel 4. The entire group was excited.

I called the station Tuesday afternoon and asked for Beth O'Connell. She said, "Reporter Dan Rea and the newsroom camera will be at your apartment at 6:00 tonight."

I couldn't thank her enough. I said, "Gee I'd love to meet you someday and have lunch."

"What do you mean meet me? You know who I am!"

Now I was on the spot. I couldn't remember her.

"This is Beth O'Connell," she said. "You know, Beth."

Well, Beth O'Connell was a name I didn't recognize, but the name Beth rang a bell. I said "Oh, no. Is this the Beth O'Connell from Westford that babysat my children for three straight winter vacations?"

"Yea, that's me! I've been following your story for a year. I've seen all the letters, articles and literature you have sent the station. I've been working with Charlie. I'm the news assignment editor. Channel 4 hired me when I graduated from UMass."

What a small world! And what a blessing to have a friend in the media!

As planned, Channel 4 arrived at 6:00 sharp. Some members of the group, including me, were quite nervous but excited. The burn survivors with noticeable facial scars were even more nervous. What would the public reaction be?

Enter cameras, film crew, and reporter Dan Rea, who we'd all seen many times on TV. We all talked for a good half hour. Dan seemed genuinely concerned. He apologized that such an important subject would only receive a one-minute spot on the late night news.

Maureen spoke of having to really work hard upon leaving the hospital. Rochelle, another friend and burn survivor, touched on the psychological adjustments burn survivors have to make. I talked about fire prevention, but John, a motorcycle burn crash victim, impressed me the most. He said, "Your face is your only mode of expression. When it becomes disfigured, it creates problems."

I was so proud of everyone. We sat around for the eleven o'clock news. Would it happen? Yes it did!

"This is Dan Rea from Weymouth, at the home of George Pessotti. George was burned in a gasoline explosion and we're here with a group of recovered burn victims celebrating a pre-Thanksgiving dinner. Major burn victims live today and face many problems. Here are the stories of a few." Then came our stories and after that, Dan concluded with, "If you are a burn victim in need of help, please contact the Brigham and Women's Hospital Burn and Trauma Unit."

A loud roar went up in my living room. We were so excited and so proud of this accomplishment. We all hugged and embraced. What a truly natural high for a worthy cause.

As a result of the story, we received calls from several burn survivors in need of help. Survivors now came from Connecticut and New Hampshire. Our efforts were being exposed to viewers all over New England. Finally, burn survivors had a place to turn for help.

Around this time I also began to put the story of my accident and the events that followed down on paper. I had heard many times in the year after the fire how therapeutic writing about such an experience can be. I had been encouraged by many people to keep a journal, but instead, I decided to do my writing in the form of a book manuscript. Once I started writing, I could not believe how easily my hand moved across the paper. The writing was, in fact, very helpful to me emotionally. I wasn't sure what I was going to do with the manuscript, but I was glad to be writing things down.

33

Soon another challenge came my way. Just a week after the WBZ taping, I was scheduled to be re-hospitalized for more corrective surgery. What would it be like? How painful would it be? What about the donor sites? These and many other questions occupied my mind.

Maureen, who had recently been in the hospital for some corrective work, was very reassuring. "It's a piece of cake," she said. "Nowhere near as painful or traumatic as our major hospitalizations."

Her reassurance helped, but I still feared the surgeon's scalpel and the anesthesia. Feeling helpless and out of control always worried me. Also, my surgery was going to be different from Maureen's. The surgeons would perform two procedures. They would remove some ugly keloid tissue under my chin, graft over this area and do an upper neck release to remove scar tissue over roughly a one by three inch area to give me more lateral movement in my neck. They would also do a contracture release of the major joint on my left arm. If successful, my neck and arm movements would be improved.

Joanne drove me to the hospital on Monday, December 3. The conversation was light and general, nothing too heavy. I knew we were both nervous. It was so comforting having Joanne come along. It always seemed that in time of need she was there. I knew that if she stayed too long we would both be in tears. We hugged and I said, "I'll see you tomorrow, Joey! I'll be okay. Don't worry, I'll be thinking of you." We kissed and parted.

Now the tests started: an EKG, blood and urine tests, chest X-rays and so on. Everything was fine. For the first time I was admitted to the new burn and trauma unit. The old Peter Bent Brigham was now a new 17-story hospital with one of the best burn and trauma staffs in the country.

It was nice returning to a ward where I knew many nurses. It felt somewhat like home. I had visited many burn patients on the ward. Now it was my turn.

I quickly slipped back into the hospital routine. Blood pressure and temperature every hour on the hour. I had no visitors the first evening. Everyone was home wishing, waiting, hoping, and praying that all would go well. Once again, friends and family were victims of fire because they were reminded of the horror that had taken place only 18 months ago. Vivid memories returned. The hurt of re-visualizing a loved one suffering brought back pain and agony to all.

The anesthesiologist arrived around 9:00 and introduced himself.

"Hello, Mr. Pessotti, my name is Dr. Wolc. I'll be your anesthesiologist tomorrow. Are you on any medication? Do you have any special problems I should be aware of?"

"No! Just one, I remember the first time I went to surgery I was sick and throwing up for two days. My fourth surgery was the best. Can you check to see what I received then?"

He assured me he would check and make things as comfortable as he could. "Don't eat or drink anything after midnight," he reminded me. "Rest up, and I'll see you tomorrow."

I was resting up, preparing myself mentally for the next day and the 12 days of hospitalization that would follow.

I was just beginning to doze off at 10:30 when my solitude was interrupted by the phone ringing. It was Anne.

"Hi Georgie. I was just checking on you, to wish you good luck tomorrow. I couldn't help but think about you."

"Gee, that was nice of you, Anne. I appreciate it."

"Oh, by the way, is anyone planning to be with you in the morning?"

"No, Joanne has to work."

"I'll be in, okay? I think someone ought to be there with you before surgery. I don't want you to be alone. Do you mind if I come in?"

"Gee, no, but what will you do with the kids?"

"Ken will see them off to school. I've already made the arrangement. Okay, I'll be there. See you in the morning."

At 6:45 the next morning, Anne walked into my room. Her eyes were sparkling and her face wore a supportive look. I quickly regressed 18 months. I remembered the countless mornings she had entered my room to visit. She was always punctual. Anne had showed me so much love and support during that 70-day hospitalization and here she was 18 months later, after separation and divorce.

I wondered why she was here. Did she feel guilty about the past? Did she truly not want me to be alone? Did she possibly still care? I did not know the answer to these questions then, but my answer would come two days later.

"Are you nervous, George?" she asked.

"Yea! I'll be happy when it's over. I'm so anxious; hopefully this will be the last time. I'm glad I'm getting this out of the way before Christmas and the New Year. I want to start the new year with flying colors."

I was scheduled for surgery at 9:00 A.M. At 8:15 the nurse walked in.

"Time for some medication," she said. "We're going to give you some morphine to relax you and a shot that will dry out your mouth so they can put in the breathing tube."

It didn't take the morphine long to work. Little by little I felt woozy. Only 18 months ago my body had a tremendous resistance to this wonder drug, but now a measly 10 milligrams had me sailing. My words were slurring, and I felt like I was floating on a cloud. I was talking up a storm with Anne. I have no recollection of what I said, but she kept smiling at me.

Escort showed up and said it was time to go to the OR. I was so relaxed these words didn't scare me. As I was wheeled down the corridor, Anne walked next to the stretcher. She never took her eyes off of me. As I reached the swinging doors where Anne could go no farther, her eyes filled with tears as she said, "Good luck."

I went to the holding area, awaiting assignment to an operating room. Finally the nurse wheeled me to this large open room. It looked so familiar, the big lights, the cleanliness, the assistants busily washing up and prepping for surgery. I remembered the narrowness of the OR table. The assistant pulled out the arm extensions from the side of the table. My arms were strapped down. All of this seemed so routine now.

Dr. Wolc, the anesthesiologist, arrived at my side. "Everything okay?"

I nodded my head.

"We'll give you a little gas to put you off to sleep."

I saw the mask approach my face very slowly.

"Breath easy, nice and easy."

I barely noticed the clean gas odor before I was off to never-never land.

Slowly my eyes opened. My immediate reaction was to question myself. Is it over? I moved slowly and I got my answer. The throbbing pain from my left thigh told me that the procedure was over. The donor sites ached as they had done before. I looked at the clock; it was 3:00 P.M. I drifted back to sleep. I kept moving between conscious and semi-conscious until finally I was out of Recovery and on my way back to my room. I don't remember being transferred to my bed.

My eyes opened and closed slowly. The people around me seemed blurred; their voices were muddled. Finally I recognized Don White and his wife, Mary. Don was a burn survivor. Eight months prior I had visited him as he struggled to survive. We had become burn friends, now he was visiting me. I felt good. I tried to talk.

"Thanks for coming. That was so nice of you," I managed to say.

I then drifted back to sleep. Around 6:30 I came to. Joanne was at my bedside staring at me. I sighed with relief.

"It's over, Joey, it's over. I'm so happy it's over."

I vaguely remember Mom and Dad standing on the other side. "We had to come to make sure you were alright. Get some rest. We love you. We'll be in soon again." Then they were gone.

I kept dozing but around 10:00 P.M., I felt much more alert. I now noticed that my left arm was in a cast from the wrist to shoulder. I could feel a heavy bandage around my throat and neck. The cast would keep my arm straight for one week until the bandages and stitches could be removed.

As usual, the grafted areas didn't hurt but the donor sites on my left thigh were driving me crazy. It was now Wednesday morning, and I decided to try and get up to urinate. As soon as I put pressure on the leg, the pain arrived in full doses. The blood rushed to my sensitive thigh that had just been stripped of skin to patch me up. I hobbled to the toilet maybe 30 feet away. I held on to the side rail trying to keep the weight off my left leg. The competition now started. The urge to urinate was overpowered by the pain on my thigh. I struggled and tried to concentrate on urinating. I thought I would pass out. Finally the urine came. What a relief! I staggered back to bed and elevated my leg.

Joanne and several of my close friends visited on a regular basis the next few days. Their love and support meant so much to me. They were always there by my side, encouraging me and sharing with me.

Thursday night arrived. The phone rang at 10:30 and awakened me. As I answered it, I had no idea how important a call this would turn out to be.

"Hello, George, how are you feeling?"

"Oh pretty good, Anne! Lots of pain on the donor sites, but I'm doing okay."

Anne's tone of voice seemed quite different—curious, inquisitive, searching. I became suspicious.

"How come you're calling, Anne? What's up?"

"Well, I've been doing a lot of thinking. I've realized I miss an awful lot of things about you. Your sense of humor, your friendship, your business dealings, our friends, our style of living. I'm wondering if we're making a mistake. I'm having second thoughts. The divorce will be final in three months. I still love you. You're so different from Ken. You're an exciting person. I miss you. Do you think we could talk about it? "

My immediate reaction was shock and dismay. I was speechless. The pain left my thighs and switched to my brain!

"I can't give you an answer to this, Anne. I'm involved with Joanne, and a lot to time has gone by. I don't know. I just don't know."

Anne rambled on but at times my mind was off in another world. I couldn't believe what I was hearing.

"I've learned a lot the last year," she said. "I've matured. I've realized the grass isn't greener on the other yard. It would be good for the kids, financially, etc. Can we talk?"

I made a commitment. "I need time to think. I'll talk to you tomorrow. Good-night."

My mind had seemed so settled the last six months. Now one phone call had raised havoc with my emotions. What's going on? Has this surgery brought back memories of the past to Anne? Was her guilt coming out? Could she really still love me? Did I still love her?

Panic set in. I felt anger! What is she doing? Maybe because of the surgery her emotions were leaking out. I had so many unanswered questions.

Again the timing seemed terrible. I can't handle this, I thought. I must be strong mentally to get strong physically. I'm not going to think about this until tomorrow. Maybe it's all a dream. Did she really call? For a time I thought the medication was raising hell with my mind. I felt out of control, with no one to talk to. I felt alone.

Naturally, I had trouble sleeping that night. The pain in my donor sites and grafted areas seemed to intensify. Was this real pain or was my mental insecurity intensifying the throbbing?

Over and over, I asked myself why this was happening...what's going on? Why has my life been so painful the last two years? What is my reason for living? Has God selected me to bear his cross, endure the world's pain? Why is this happening? There has to be a reason. I felt so unsettled.

At times, as we all do, I got angry with God. I questioned His motives. What have I done to offend You? I've lived a good clean life. I'm a good father. I enjoy helping people. I work hard. I'm not an alcoholic or a drug addict. I think I'm a good person. Why has this happened to me? For the first time in my life I started to seriously question my existence. What is my purpose in life? Where am I going? I started to soul search. At times I would apologize to God. I'm sorry I questioned You. I guess I have to thank You for my life. You gave me life. You gave me Joanne, a caring loving family, friends, and two beautiful children. I should be happy and I am. But please let up on me. Give me a break!

34

The morning brought a new day full of the regular routines that I had mastered in my first hospitalization: blood tests, urine test, IV Lines, temps and blood pressures. Dr. Mulliken, Dr. Murray, and five residents walked in at 6:00 A.M. I often wondered if doctors ever slept.

Dr. Murray, one of the best plastic surgeons in Boston, was explaining to the residents the surgical procedures that had been performed on me. He explained the contracture release on my left arm.

"Heavy scar tissue was restricting Mr. Pessotti's joint movement. It was like trying to bend a steel pipe; all the tension was in the middle. The reason we cut half way around his arm is obvious. If you try to bend that steel rod and can't, then you cut it a little and then a little more. The pipe will not bend in half until you have cut the pipe exactly in half or 180 degrees. Now the pipe or arm can bend freely, back and forth."

The procedure made sense. I couldn't wait for the cast and bandages to come off. What would my arm and neck look like? Would there be improvement? Would the ugly scars on my neck be gone?

"Rest up, Mr. Pessotti. We will remove the bandages next week," the doctor said.

I was anxious for the scarlet red bandages on my thigh to come off. I knew from the past it would take seven to 10 days. I also knew that after seven days most of the pain would disappear because a fresh new layer of skin was developing. I kept the sunlamp on the damp scarlet bandages every four hours. This helped dry out the oozing body secretions that could cause infection under the bandages. The warmth felt good.

As the day wore on I started thinking of the phone call from Anne. She would be here at 3:00. What would happen? I began to get nervous.

At 3:10 I could hear the familiar scuffling of little shoes coming down the hallway. I knew it was Anne with Stephen in one hand and David in the other. My suspicions were confirmed. Six quizzical eyes entered room 11A. It seemed like minutes before any words were spoken. I could feel their eyes wandering over my body. Their eyes moved up and down the cast on my left arm and up to the "plug like" bandages that were stitched to my neck.

A quiet, concerned Anne said, "How are you doing, George?"

"Okay, Anne, okay. A little sore but fine."

Steve and Dave came over and kissed me on the cheek. They were always a little shy while visiting me in the hospital. I'm sure their little minds were also flashing back to the long hospitalization. Then the usual flood of questions started.

"Why is the cast on your arm, Dad? Does it hurt? What are those funny looking bandages on your neck? How long will you be here? Will you sleep alone tonight? Will those scars go away?"

I don't remember if I ever answered them all. The important factor was to assure them that I was okay. "I love you, kids. I miss you. I can't wait to come home. I'll be okay." Constant reassurance is what the kids needed and I never forgot that.

I felt I was talking a lot and rambling. Maybe subconsciously I was trying to control the conversation so Anne couldn't speak. The superficial conversation soon came to an end when Anne asked, "Have you given any thought to my call the other night?"

"Well, kinda. I'm confused. I'm not sure. Why bring this up now?"

"Well, I've been doing a lot of thinking. I feel I've changed a lot. I've had a year and a half and several relationships. I really feel I've given up a good thing. I love Ken but he's a lot different than you. I miss your excitement, enthusiasm, and successes. You've shown me how much you love the kids. They adore the ground you walk on. I really think we could make it as a family if we really tried. I'm willing to work at it. I wasn't willing to work at it before. I was screwed up at the time of your accident. I feel I've matured. I realized the important things in life are family and togetherness. My father's illness and cancer has made me think of the finer things in life."

"Well, I thought you didn't love me; that's why I left home. You said you didn't love me. Now you do? I don't understand. "

"I always did love you, George. I just couldn't sort out the important things in our relationship. There are a lot of qualities about you that I miss and that I love. It could be so good for all of us if our marriage could work out."

I was well aware of the advantages to the kids and the financial benefits. But that wasn't the most important thing to me. The kids had adjusted. I had adjusted. Our finances had adjusted. The two most important questions were did Anne really love me or only miss me and did I still love Anne?

I knew I had loved Anne at the time of our breakup. Many of the feelings were still there. They hadn't totally gone away. I knew I could still love her. My love, dedication, and feelings for Anne were never in doubt for eight years of marriage. It was Anne who questioned her love for me and decided she didn't want to stay married.

The risks of reconciling were many, but the rewards could be plentiful. We talked on and off over the next 10 days of my hospitalization. I was trying to test Anne's feelings. Was she serious or was she again mixed up emotionally? The intensity of our conversations indicated to me that she was quite serious. She desperately wanted a marriage that she had thrown away 18 months ago.

Only seven days ago my life was relatively settled. I had Joanne, whom I loved very much. I was struggling to rebuild my life with her as a major part of it.

And now, unexpectedly, Annie wanted to get back together. All of a sudden my life was in a frenzy, a merry-go-round of emotions. I felt panicky.

Did I still love Anne? Should I love her after all she had put me through? Should I even consider reconciling? What about Joanne? What about family and friends? I knew the pressure from them would be tremendous because many people were still furious with Anne for seeking a divorce at such an unfortunate time in my life.

Something inside me told me I had to find out if there was any hope for Anne and me. I felt the door had been left open a crack. Being a decisive person, I felt the door had to swing open or be slammed shut once and forever. It couldn't stay open a crack. My life could not go forward while this issue was in limbo. Indecision I've always felt is the biggest robber of opportunity.

I decided to make a firm decision but not right away. I wanted to test the water. Maturity had taught me to walk before I ran. I could not share this news with anyone. I had a lot of soul searching and thinking to do. I would not make any rash decisions. After all I still had some physical healing to do. I still had seven days of bed rest ahead of me. I was also anxious to have my bandages removed.

I now felt uneasiness inside me every time Joanne visited. Should I tell her my feelings? Should I remain silent, knowing that maybe the whole ordeal would blow over? Were my emotions showing? Would she suspect something was wrong?

Part of me felt I was being unfaithful to Joanne just by thinking about the possibility of returning to Anne. Life just seemed so unkind, so unsettling to me. Beginning with the two trial separations from Anne, I had struggled for over two years for stability and now instability and indirection had returned. When would it end? Would it ever end? Will I ever find my purpose in life, my reason for living?

35

My immediate goal was to get my bandages off, check the results of the surgery, and get home for the Christmas holiday. I knew I was healing because the stitches were starting to itch, and the swelling in my arm was subsiding because the cast was starting to slide up and down my arm. The scarlet red bandage on my thigh was starting to dry out, and the incessant pain had now been reduced to a dull ache. I knew my release was coming soon. Soon, Dr. Sharon Bushnell confirmed my diagnosis.

"We'll take the cast and bandages off tomorrow," she told me. I couldn't wait to see what the surgeon's scalpel had performed. My shock and surprise came at 6:00 the next morning. Dr. Bushnell walked in with a Black and Decker saber saw. The high pitch whining sound reminded me of a dentist's drill. In an instant the cast was in two pieces. It felt so good just getting rid of that extra 15 pounds.

Now for the plug-like bandages. I had never seen a bandage stitched on. The stitches were holding the plug-like bandage to the base of the wound. A few more snips and the bandage dropped off.

My jaw dropped when I looked at my now exposed arm. Half my arm was gone! It looked like I had a shrapnel metal wound. There was a canyon with a thin piece of skin from my thigh covering the arteries and muscles. I could see a vein pulsating under the infant graft.

In walked Dr. Mulliken. He instantly saw the concern on my face.

"Will this stay like this, John?" I asked.

"Oh no! That's a beautiful graft. Look here, bend your arm."

I could immediately feel more range of motion.

"As the wound heals it will thicken and push up. You'll see; in a few weeks most of the ridges will be gone."

He explained that the wound was like fresh dough waiting to rise. "In time it will come up," he said.

I knew John hadn't misled me in the past. His words were comforting.

"Okay, let's look at that neck," I said.

This wound looked the same but not so shocking. The bump-like nodules that were so ugly and difficult to shave around were now gone.

They were replaced with a new flat like graft. Cosmetically, they looked great. My neck was an obvious area that people stared at. Hopefully now the grafts would discourage future curiosity seekers.

A nice release graft was inserted below the nodule replacement graft. This would greatly help my range of movement in my neck, especially left to right and over the shoulder movement. Little by little the surgeons were tuning my engine, making minor adjustments here and there.

I couldn't wait to shave off the seven-day beard I had grown while recuperating. My left arm seemed so heavy I could hardly lift it to my face. I was so excited about the new grafts that the 25 minutes it took me to shave went by quite rapidly. I felt so spiffy. Clean hair, clean shave, almost ready to go home.

As a burn survivor I took pride in showing my graft to the other burn survivors I had become friends with. Maureen and Rochelle came to visit, and we shared our experiences, further strengthening our common supportive bond. Only weeks before Maureen had reassured me that this hospitalization would be nothing like our initial stay. She was right. Now having gone through it, I genuinely thanked her for providing me with that reassurance. Our excitement seemed to buoy Rochelle, who would face surgery next. Having a support group was definitely working for me and for both of them.

I would go home the next day. Step by step, inch by inch, piece by piece, my physical being was being put back together. It was never to be the same, but it was so much improved over what it had been in the days and weeks right after the fire.

My emotional pressure seemed to outweigh my physical encumbrances. The year-end holidays were fast approaching. The emotional battle continued to be waged inside me. Joanne and I were in the midst of planning a Caribbean vacation, something we both deserved and needed. The Christmas presents were mounting under the tree.

Again, the timing seemed so bad. Christmas has so much special meaning. It was a time to be with loved ones. Before Anne brought up the possibility of reconciling, I had looked forward to the coming holiday as my first real Christmas in two years. Now it seemed certain to be doomed by emotional turmoil, no matter what choice I made.

I still had a lot of uncertainty about Anne. Something inside told me there was still a chance for us. Could I still love her? I seemed more certain about my feelings; I knew that, as in the past, if I committed to her, I would live up to that commitment.

Anne seemed to be so sure of her feelings. Our two separations prior to the fire had not been effective in helping her resolve the confusion in her mind. Maybe, just maybe, this last year was a true separation that gave her the space to truly understand what she wanted.

Can people really change? Can incompatibility suddenly turn to compatibility? Could the concerns about the kids and finances be clouding major issues?

Somehow I felt distant from Joanne. This pending reconciliation was driving me crazy. I was obsessed. The bubble had to burst. Would or should I risk my relationship with Joanne? I was now acting on emotions, not logic. The next two months would prove to be a roller coaster ride. Some would be survivors; others would become victims.

I now faced a heavyweight fight. In one corner was Anne, former champion of my emotions. When she asked for a divorce, she had decided to quit boxing. She threw in the towel. She gave up. The pressures in the ring were too much for her. Now suddenly she wanted a rematch, a taste of something she told me she missed.

In the other corner was Joanne, a true fighter and champion. She was the underdog who had worked her way to the top. She had mastered her emotions for me. Her victory had only come from persistence. She had been knocked down so many times. Did she have what it would take to withstand one more trip into the ring?

The next two months would bring loads of speculation from onlookers on the outside of this battle. Wagers were placed. The arena would be crowded with spectators taking sides. Someone would lose. Someone would win. And what would I be—a winner or a loser?

36

I checked out of the hospital 12 days after my surgery with nowhere near the trauma that accompanied my previous release from the hospital. I was much stronger physically, but the memories of hospital rooms, operating tables, nurses, medications, and procedures were ever so similar, routines I would never forget.

Joanne was there to drive me to Weymouth. The excitement of my successful surgery was shadowed by my emotional turmoil. It didn't take Joanne long to figure out that something was bothering me. I wasn't my fun loving self. I knew I couldn't cover my feelings forever. I'd always had a policy of honesty with Joanne. As I often said, "You might get angry with me, you may even hate me, but you will always respect me for being honest." I had been brought up on that theory and I believed in it.

Less than 36 hours after I returned home, Mt. St. Helen's erupted between Joanne and me. It was the start of a battle of courage, love, fear, anger, and indecision.

Joanne was very perceptive. On Wednesday evening, she began to ask me, "What's on your mind? Is something bothering you? Do you feel okay?"

I finally mustered enough energy to blow it out. "Jo, I really don't know where to begin," I said. "You've noticed the last two weeks that I've been distant emotionally. You are right. I'm struggling with a decision. Anne has been having second thoughts about our divorce. She feels she still loves me. She says she's made a mistake."

No immediate response. Just a look of emptiness, confusion, hurt, frustration—you name it, Joanne's face showed it.

Finally, she spoke. "Well, what do you think? How do you feel? What about us? How could she? Where does that leave me?"

I had few answers for her.

"I'm not jumping to any conclusions. It's something I'm not sure of. I think I still love Anne. It's something I have to find out."

"How can you do this? I thought our relationship was going strong. Why does she love you now? She didn't love you 18 months ago when she threw you out of the house. She wasn't there when you really needed her. What makes it so different now? I've been with you through thick and think. I've always been second fiddle. I'm sick of it."

It was now midnight. Suddenly, Joanne said, "I'm leaving."

"Where are you going?"

"I'm going out."

I was now scared. I had never seen Joanne so distraught. Would she come back? My worry was reinforced by what she said next.

"I'm going to get a pack of cigarettes."

Joanne had quit smoking four months ago, and now I had given her a reason to start again.

"I'll be right back," she reassured me.

Joanne was gone for ten minutes and it seemed like an eternity. Had I lost my best friend? Was this the last straw? Was I cracking up?

When Joanne returned our conversation continued.

"How can you even consider going back?" she asked.

"I have to find out, Joanne. I can't go forward with my life or our life until I find out."

My mind kept wandering to utopia. Wouldn't it be great for the kids? I missed them so much. Also, if our marriage could work, there would be tremendous financial advantages. Could the good times for Anne and me return? Feelings deep inside told me I still loved her, but could we forget the past? So much hurt and so much time had elapsed.

Joanne just could not understand my thinking. Deep down inside I think she knew why I had to find out. I always felt Joanne didn't totally understand because she didn't have any children from her marriage. Often times I felt I had disappointed Stephen and David. Part-time parenthood was something I had never bargained for. I so much wanted to be with them and watch them grow. As a person I never could accept failure. My marriage had failed. Was there a chance to turn it around–a chance to restore success?

My news, of course, dampened the Christmas spirit for Joanne. Only a year before she had been disenchanted as I spent Christmas Day with Anne, Steve, and Dave. This year Joanne had been excited about our Christmas. Quickly the presents under the tree lost meaning. Joanne barked, "Why couldn't you wait until after Christmas? Did you have to spoil everything?"

Somehow that night ended and moonlight soon turned to sunrise. Thank God my surgery had given me a reprise from work. I don't think

I could have handled business pressure with the emotional strain I was experiencing.

Anne and I had agreed that instead of taking the boys to my place on weekends, I would try spending the weekends in Westford. This would give us time to talk seriously about the future. I was looking forward to my first weekend "home." I was anxious but cautious.

Friday night came and as usual I tucked the kids into bed. We said our prayers and thanked God for our blessings. The kids had sensed a change in the atmosphere.

Stephen asked, "Dad, do you love my Mom? Are you moving back home?"

"I don't know, Steve; Mom and I have a lot of talking to do." I was impressed with his astuteness.

"If you move home, Dad, can I help you?" David blurted. "You'll need a big truck."

I couldn't help but get excited by their excitement, but I also didn't want to disappoint them. They had experienced more than their share of that emotion already in their short lives.

Anne and I talked until at least 2:00 A.M. Everything seemed to be fitting together. She told me how much she loved me and, for the first time in several years, I felt she meant it, but I still couldn't figure why.

"What will you do about Ken? You say you love him too."

"We're not jumping into anything. I've been honest with him; he knows my feelings. If we get back together, he'll just have to accept it. I've really had some time to analyze my true feelings. There are a lot of qualities in you I like and miss. Your sense of humor, your honesty, your hard work, success, your love for the kids and so on. Somehow I couldn't see it before. I was all screwed up. I didn't know what I wanted or what I was looking for."

Anne confided that when I came home from the hospital she had been in love with Leo, the insurance agent I had overheard her arguing with the day they had gone together to pick up the final insurance check. The net result was that he was married with two kids and not about to leave home. Anne had chased him for months only to come up short. She had never chased me; I was always there. She said she was finally over Leo and realized she had made a mistake.

I was still struggling to remain cautious. I was risking a sure relationship with Joanne for a long shot with Anne. I agreed that we would continue to see each other two or three times a week. Nice and easy, step by step. I felt in time I would know the answer.

We agreed not to sleep together until a decision was made. The kids had become used to seeing Ken there in the mornings, and we didn't want to confuse them further. I had just settled into the double bed in the guestroom when Anne came in.

"If we're going to get back together," she said, "I want to be honest and above board with you. I have something to tell you. When we were going through the divorce you threatened me one night when I was drunk. You said you would take the kids away from me if my drinking continued. I got scared. The next day I went to the bank and withdrew $10,000 from the fire insurance account and re-deposited it in an account in my name. I've felt guilty about this for over a year."

I was shocked! "How could you? After what I went through, you stole $10,000? How could you?"

"I was frightened. I thought I would need the money for any attorney to keep my kids. I didn't want to lose them. You threatened me."

"Well, I respect your honesty, but it was wrong."

"I know. I'm sorry. I just had to tell you. Please forgive me."

"Well, I don't know about you, Anne, but I've had it for one night. Let's get some rest; we'll continue tomorrow." We embraced, kissed and went to sleep in separate rooms.

The next morning I was awakened by a little body nuzzling next to me. David had climbed in bed with me. He had put his little arm around me and fallen to sleep. Next I was awakened by Stephen, the other little tycoon.

And then as usual the questions started.

"Dad, are you moving back home?"

"I'm not sure, Steve."

"Well, is it yes or no?"

"I said maybe."

"Well, does maybe mean yes?"

"Well, Steve, most of the time that I tell you maybe, it means yes, because I miss you guys a lot and I don't like always saying no."

"Well, is it more yes or more no?"

"Well, Steve, I think the answer is more yes."

"Well, if it's more yes, then will you move home in the spring time or the summer time?" I could not believe the precision and logic this six-year-old possessed. He was on a relentless pursuit to obtain a yes—a chance, a hope that his dad may be home for good.

Saturday morning brought memories of past marital years, including a nice breakfast consisting of poached eggs, bacon, toast, juice and coffee and errands such as the dump, the bank, and grocery shopping.

Suddenly Sunday arrived and it was time to leave. Anne knew I had to go, but Steve and David didn't understand.

"When will I see you again?" Anne asked.

"I'll be out Wednesday as usual."

"I'll miss you, George," Anne said. "Keep in touch; we will continue talking next week."

We embraced and slowly I walked away. So many fond memories, so many tragic ones, the walls seemed to whisper secrets. The neighbors watched in wonder, no doubt asking each other why my car was there for two nights.

I felt many emotions as I drove away. I had felt much love; I had also given and received it. The kids were great, but somehow something was missing. I was still searching for my purpose in life, my reason for living.

My mind wandered as my '77 T-Bird cruised the lonely 60 miles to Weymouth. Joanne would await me. I felt in limbo. I wanted to give so much to her, but couldn't. My emotions were being bulldozed all over.

37

If I had only stopped to realize what I had done to Joanne, I would have understood the cold reception I received when I got to Weymouth. My mind was still spinning from the weekend. Now I was thrust into another emotional situation. Joanne naturally had a million questions, and God knows she deserved the answers.

I was trying to play the middle. It wasn't working. I wanted both women but was lost in uncertainty and indecision. One thing for sure, I couldn't handle the emotional and physical commitment of two relationships. The bubble would inevitably burst, and I bore all the risks. Maybe I would be left all alone. I might strike out twice.

Soon Christmas was only a day away. Joanne and I had many social commitments to live up to, with both Christmas and New Year's Eve parties. But the excitement and sparkle of the season was overshadowed by the impending nightmarish soap opera.

We went through the motions. I missed Joanne's closeness, emotional understanding, and loving for the first time in our relationship. My true feelings for Joanne were being tested. So many times I had unconsciously taken her for granted. Now she was gone, gone emotionally and gone physically as the intimate part of our relationship came to a halt.

Joanne and I spent Christmas Eve together. We both blessed each other with many fine gifts. But the true love and meaning of Christmas was gone that evening. I felt so rotten. Why was this happening? Just two weeks ago our lives seemed to be settling down.

I visited Mom and Dad for our traditional Christmas dinner. As I sat through dinner I wondered how Mom and Dad would feel about the possible reconciliation with Anne. Somehow deep inside my uneasiness gave me my answer. Sooner or later they would find out. Anne had already confided in her parents, who were in Arizona for the winter. They were ecstatic about the decision. Anne's family rallied behind her. I had always known how much her family loved me. They were all visibly shaken when our marriage crumbled. Now they, like me, were hoping things would work out.

I knew my future was in my hands, but I struggled for the guiding light. Pressure was building internally because Anne and I hadn't shared our possible reconciliation with many people. I didn't want to burden friends and families. I had to wrestle with this one on my own. I suddenly realized how important friends are. If you can't turn to them and share your joys, sorrows, problems and fears, then what are friends for?

I sampled a couple of close friends. Frank Quinn, one of my best friends, was not judgmental; he listened and tried to understand me. He didn't criticize or condemn like many people soon would. He didn't consider his feelings above mine, like many people would. His concern, love, and friendship were genuine.

"George, I'll be your friend regardless of your decision," he said simply. His words were so comforting. But for the most part I would remain silent for another month, watching, waiting, wishing, and hoping.

Two major obstacles to the reconciliation occurred in a short span. Joanne and I had planned a February vacation in the Caribbean. Would we or should we go? I have always been a fanatic about keeping commitments. We had planned and decided to go a long time ago. That decision I would not change. Perhaps it would be my last vacation or my last days and hours with Joanne. Somehow I needed that time desperately. We went forward with our plans.

Early in January Anne's father had a relapse with cancer. His previous operations were unsuccessful; the cancer had spread. His days surely seemed numbered. Anne called me on a Sunday evening; she was naturally distraught.

"Daddy's dying. I'm flying to Arizona in the morning. Ken will help with the kids, the Resniks will help, and can you help as much as you can?"

Here was another obstacle in our marriage reconciliation. Inevitably, this trip to Arizona, which Anne initially anticipated would last a few days, turned into weeks. I understood that Anne had to be with her father, that this time was important to her, but I also felt cheated. After all, wasn't our future important too?

Constant detours sidetracked the reconciliation process. Some people might conjecture that these were omens, signs from the universe that we were headed down the wrong road. If this was the case, both of us blindly ignored them.

I continued to speak with Anne frequently while she was in Arizona. Our chief topic of conversation was John, my father-in-law. One day he seemed good, then another day incoherent. He flashed back at times to his childhood. Often he either didn't recognize Anne or thought she was his wife, Nancy. It was a very tough situation for Anne.

Two weeks passed and John was still hanging on. Anne called one night and said she wanted to stay to the end. I felt a lot of anger. Why wasn't anyone else in Anne's family out there helping? If I had thought about this question a little closer, I would have known the answer. John had done a fine job of alienating his six children. In his later years he had mellowed and spoke of his love for his children, but the fact remained that for 30 years his cantankerous ways never allowed him to show his kids the love they truly deserved. He had been a workaholic and an alcoholic. He lost thousands of inherited dollars in a family woodworking business. His four sons were embittered and alienated.

Anne sensed I was upset with her decision to stay. I said, "You're right, Anne; I am disappointed. There you are out in Arizona, the kids are being bounced around the neighborhood, and our marriage and future have again been put on the back burner. Don't you care? Isn't your family and life important?"

"Please don't ask me to come home. I have to be here with Daddy; he needs me. Mom is all alone out here. Please bear with it."

I tried to put myself in her shoes and understand. I supposed if it were my father I would also want to be at his side.

I decided to take four days off from work to give the kids a little stability. Ken had been super with the kids. He took time off from work, saw the kids off to school every morning, did laundry, and cooked for them. He was doing a superb job of mother and father. One Wednesday evening when I was with the boys Ken stopped by for coffee and a chat. So many memories flashed back as I sat in my rocking chair next to the fireplace. A warm cracking fire dulled January's impact on a chilled family room. What an odd situation, I thought, to sit here in my former home and calmly share a cup of coffee with my former wife's lover.

Ken and I sipped our coffee and Cointreau. The superficial conversation soon turned serious.

"George, I want to tell you something. If you and Anne get back together, I want you to know I won't stand in the way. I know you love Anne. I also love her, but I will back off if she decides to go back with you. It will be hard, but I will adjust. I would like to be friends; we have all shared so much. I would like to be able to stay friends with Anne, maybe an occasional drink.

I give you my word as a friend, that if you're back with Anne I will never go to bed with her again."

We both held back tears. We both knew the hurt of losing a loved one. Only a year ago Ken had lost his wife to cancer and their four boys were his lifelong responsibility. I marveled at Ken's honesty. Often times he reminded me of myself. He had put his love for Anne in second place. It was a love that was so strong that he would step aside for her happiness. His words were a strong witness of his love for her. A firm handshake and a soft pat on the shoulder ended our conversation that cold winter night.

Pressure was mounting to tell my parents and family that Anne and I were considering a reconciliation. I decided to test the waters. Little did I know that sharks were awaiting me. Unbeknownst to me, my parents had been suspicious for weeks. Call it parental intuitiveness if you will, but they weren't surprised. By phone I tried to explain or justify this crucial decision. At first I did all the talking.

"Anne has changed," I explained. "She feels she made a mistake. Won't it be better for the kids?"

All of my key rehearsed lines were not budging my parents.

"I'm sorry," my father said. "It will never be the same. Son, love is not like a faucet; you can't turn it on and off at will. Anne didn't love you two years ago. I don't believe she could love you now."

I hung up. I was so hurt. Why couldn't they at least be supportive? They acted like they were hurt more than me by the divorce. It's my life, my decision! But without family support, I knew I faced a tough road ahead. Some associates, friends, and family members were supportive; I assumed the ones who said nothing were unsupportive. I now had one more issue to think over.

Joanne and I continued our planning for going to St. Croix. I needed a break. My father said, "If you're getting together with Anne, then how come you're going on vacation with Joanne?"

He had a good point. But Joanne and I both needed a change. Unfortunately, our vacation was drudgery. Each passing day brought the agony of knowing that our relationship might end after the vacation when I returned to Anne, who arrived home from Arizona the day after Joanne and I left on our vacation. That effectively postponed the decision for two more weeks.

Thank God our vacation was spent with eight good friends. There was always a laugh, good food, good beaches, and good company.

Our good friends, Dick and Natalie from Martha's Vineyard, couldn't believe my decision. Dick said, "I don't understand. Joanne is so good to you. You will never find someone who loves you as much as she does. She worships the ground you walk on. How can you love Anne after two years? I have been divorced twice; after two years I didn't love my ex-wives. If anything I hated them! I hope you know what you are doing."

Each day of vacation became harder emotionally. Joanne was withdrawing from me totally. We slept together but that was about all. Our loving kisses had turned into routine good night kisses, our warm embraces had fizzled to cold stares and daydreams, our lovemaking was purely physical. For the first time in my life I saw a heart being broken right in front of me and I was the cause. It hurt so much. Why was I turning away my savior... my lifeline to the future? Was my love for Anne so blind? Was I basing my decision on fact or emotion? Was I chasing something only because I knew I couldn't have it?

I was saddened three days before our vacation ended, when I learned that my father-in-law had died. He had clung to life for 3,000 miles, a journey from Arizona to Massachusetts in his Winnebago, with two of his sons at his side. He knew he was going home to die. The suffering was over. It was another cross for Anne to bear, another loss in the young lives of Stephen and David, and, ultimately, another nail in the coffin to our future.

38

We arrived home from St. Croix on Tuesday, February 17, 1981. The next five days would change my life forever. Wednesday, my first day back in the office, played havoc with my emotions. Joanne, who was also my secretary, was now totally ignoring me. The hurt was too much for her; she couldn't even face me. I was so hurt as she walked by my office, time after time, not even nodding to acknowledge my existence. Her actions tightened her hold on my emotions. I had lost my right arm, my co-pilot, my navigator, my rudder. I was lost and adrift at sea. I needed love and support so much; logic went out the window as I operated only on emotions.

I couldn't wait to get to Westford. I hadn't seen Anne in six weeks or the kids in two weeks. Now that my father-in-law was dead, was the road clear for our reconciliation? Was I anxious because of my loss of Joanne? Was my future waiting there or was I doomed? I had trouble pinpointing my excitement.

As I pulled into the driveway Stephen and David jumped for joy. Their mom was home and now their dad was home. We hugged and kissed as cold February tears ran down my face. As I looked up there was Anne. We embraced for what seemed like hours. There was so much to say and so many questions to ask, but our lips could not quiver a word. Thoughts were passing through our brains like the fast rewind button on a tape recorder had been pushed.

"It's so good to see you, Anne," I said. "I'm so sorry about your father. At least he's not suffering anymore. How was the funeral?"

"It was so sad but beautiful. Reverend Knight said the service at the old Episcopal Church in Clinton. The whole family was there. Mom hasn't shed a tear through this whole ordeal. I hope she doesn't crack."

"How about you, Anne?"

"I'm okay. I haven't been sleeping; it was so sad to see Dad wither away. I'm so happy I went to Arizona. I hope you can understand. I had to be with Daddy. I kept a diary for three weeks, with so many things Dad said I will never forget."

"I'm glad your father didn't die here in front of Steve and Dave. It would have been just another hurdle. I didn't think would be good for them."

A few weeks back Anne had discussed moving her father into the Westford house until they could find a nursing home. I was vehemently opposed to this on two fronts. Number one, it would be a big interference on our marriage reconciliation, and number two, I didn't want the kids to see their grandfather wither away pound by pound.

"How was St. Croix?"

"The weather was fine and the company was good. It was a real emotional two weeks for Joanne and me. It's almost like each day was a slow death for our relationship, because it came to an end. I'll really miss her. It's hard to be just friends when we've shared so much. I think Joanne will quit work soon. I really feel bad the way things ended."

"How do Gail and Doug and Dick and Natalie feel?"

"Well, I think you know the answers. Gail and Doug don't say much. They're supportive regardless of our decision. Dick and Nat can't believe it. We've become very close the last two years. Dick told me that I'd never find anyone who loves me as much as Joanne. He thinks I'm crazy. Oh, well, we can't live our lives wondering what other people think; they're already think it."

"How about your mother and father?" she asked.

I had to tone down their unsupportive comments because I knew it would be uncomfortable for Anne. "My mother and father said things will be difficult, but they'll try their best."

Anne seemed to be quizzing me, looking for support for her decision.

"I think we should continue as planned and see what happens," I said to reassure her. "I've made a commitment to spend time with you to see where our relationship is going. I can't be involved with you and Joanne at the same time. I've made that decision. It's too emotionally and physically draining. I can't take it. How about you and Ken? What's going on?"

"He knows. He's been very emotional. He cries a lot. It hasn't been easy. He loves me a lot, but still wants to be friends. Can you handle that, my seeing Ken once and awhile? Nothing physical, just friends?"

Deep down inside I wanted to say no, even though Ken had reassured me of his intentions. I still felt very insecure. Old memories of past insecurities about Anne's infidelity quickly surfaced. I struggled to relegate past mistakes to the past, but somehow they seemed relevant for the future.

"I suppose it's okay, Anne."

"It's hard to just break off our relationship. I've become a mother to Ken's youngest boy, Kenny. He's having a hard time since his mother died. I just can't shut him off. These things will take time, but they will work out."

I still felt as though my life was up in the air. I planned to keep my apartment in Weymouth; I didn't want to leap into anything.

Over the next two days Anne and I tried discussing issues—our future together, our assets and, most of all, our liabilities. Had the problems of our marriage gone away? For the first time in ages I felt that Anne did love me. Somehow this seemed to solve many of our previous problems, but I still didn't feel secure.

I tried to sum up my situation as I saw it for Anne. "We've both changed, Anne," I told her. "You're more independent and so am I. I'm doing many things right now that are important to me. For the first time in my life, I've thought about me. I'm trying to find my reason for living. As you know I'm very involved with The Phoenix Society. We're just completing filming a TV special, 'Where There's Smoke,' that will air in April. I'm real proud of that show. It's like a dream come true being on television but more important is that I'm spreading the word that burn survivors truly need support and recognition.

"Also, as you know, I'm writing a book and things are going well with that," I continued. "I'm making some publishing contacts; there's talk of a possible movie. Business is also going well and I'm quite busy. I believe that the quality of time I'll spend with you and the kids will be better. You know I can't be here seven nights a week. I have too many friends and associates that are competing for pieces of time with me. I can't and won't give up all of these activities."

"I won't want you to, Georgie. I've noticed how happy you are. I'm proud of all the things you're doing. I hope you continue your special time with the kids; they really love you and worship the ground you walk on. You've been so faithful to them."

We talked about many issues. I just hoped and prayed that this time Anne could truly accept me for me, for a true ingredient of love is acceptance. Not trying to change someone for your own benefit is essential to a relationship, yet attempting to change a spouse is a classic error that often leads to divorce.

Dealing with Joanne every day at work became almost impossible. I began to miss all the favors and work Joanne did for me. I now realized that a large part of her efforts were because of love. I had lost a typist for my book and for my personal letters. I clearly saw that business-wise, I had taken Joanne for granted. Isn't it a shame in life that we don't appreciate things until they're gone?

To complicate matters even more my business partner told me he was thinking of letting Joanne go. Their personalities had gotten to the point where they frequently clashed. He felt a change was imminent. I explained to Dick that if he let Joanne go now, the whole office would suspect that I conspired with him to let her go because I was moving back with Anne. This will create a lot of hard feeling among the work force. I encouraged Dick to be tactful and cautious and to reconsider his decision.

Another associate, Dick Pratt, was skeptical about the wisdom of my reconciling with Anne, but he was not judgmental. One day, he relayed a story to me that to this day remains vivid in my mind.

"George, you know I love you as a person and friend, but let me tell you something straight on. My ex-wife Arlene just remarried. I was visiting my kids last week, and as I was sitting on the couch I observed Arlene say to Jim, her new husband, 'Jim, could you get me a cup of tea? Jim, could you lower the TV? Jim, did you switch the laundry? Jim, will you run to the store for milk?'"

Dick explained that he had flashed back 15 years to when Arlene was ordering him around. Dick said, "George, let me tell you something. That was 15 years ago, and, guess what, Arlene has *not* changed; she's the same. People don't change. I can't believe Anne has changed as much as you say. Just remember what I say; people don't change. Be careful."

In the end, Dick was so right, of course, but again my emotions were in control, not my logic, and I couldn't see the truth.

39

nne and I had planned a busy weekend. I thought it would be nice to take my mother-in-law and the Resniks to dinner on Saturday night. They all had been so great and supportive. They all were ecstatic about the prospect of my return.

Friday arrived and I was looking forward to relaxing. Emotionally, the pressure of losing Joanne and of getting the cold shoulder from her every day was both hurting and driving me crazy.

I figured I had to talk to her. I invited her to dinner Friday night. I was concerned for her well being. We agreed to meet at our favorite Chinese restaurant, the China Pavilion in Weymouth. I trudged through the pouring rain to meet Joanne at 6:00. My plans were to head for Westford after dinner.

Joanne had arrived a little early and was two vodka and grapefruits ahead of me. It had been only three days since I had last spoken to her, but it seemed like an eternity.

Near the end of the dinner, Joanne said I was really doing her a big favor by choosing Anne. I was astonished and asked her what she meant by that.

"Well, I look at it this way, George," she said. "You're not the man I thought you were; you're a weak person. Anne rings the bell and you run to Westford. You drop me and run. I decided you did me a favor because I don't want to be involved with a weak person. You now have Anne, and, believe me, you two deserve each other. You're two losers."

Joanne was both hurting me and pissing me off. Good thing dinner was ending because I was ready to leave. Through the whole meal, Joanne seemed so cocky and secure, somewhat happy over my decision. It kind of threw me; I didn't expect it.

I said, "Well, I've heard enough from you. I'm leaving. I'll see you at work on Monday." "Oh, no, you won't."

"Why not?"

"I quit today. I'm all done. I'm leaving tomorrow on a plane."

"Just like that, Jo? Seven years of working for a company, no notice, you just quit? You can't run away from life's problems; they'll always be there."

"I don't care; I can't stand it anymore."

I was heartbroken. This was probably the last time I'd ever see Joanne. What a tragic way to end a beautiful relationship. The past two years seemed so vivid. I was losing my best friend, my lover, the woman who stuck with me through two separations, the fire, the divorce, the Lanolin rubs, the ups and downs. She had been with me for the better and the worse, the sickness and the health and almost the death do us part.

My heart was broken and I couldn't stop the tears that were racing down my cheeks. I felt so cheated and lost at the thought of losing Joanne this way. She deserved better. I said goodbye and slowly turned towards the door, again struggling to hold the tears. I walked through the pouring rain to my car, happy that the rain against my face hid my tears.

As I looked over my shoulder I saw Joanne walking to her car. I backed my car out, and, out of habit, I looked to make sure her car started. No taillights, no head lights. I waited and waited. Still nothing. I backed my car up. There stood Joanne in the pouring rain standing outside her car drenched. I hopped out.

As tears streamed down her face she said, "Can't find my keys."

We searched for a moment and found them at the bottom of her pocketbook. She looked me in the face and said, "Is this how you're going to leave me? Please stay the night with me, just this last night before I leave. Please!"

"Jo, I'd love to but I've made a commitment to Anne. I have to find out. I'd be starting on the wrong foot. One night would lead to another and another and another. Can't you understand?"

"Please, I need you tonight. I've never asked you for anything, but tonight I need you. After all I've done for you and you're going to leave me like this."

I felt so guilty, but what could I do? I had made a commitment and I would live up to it.

"I'm leaving, Jo."

"You're not!"

"I am!"

"You're not." Joanne grabbed my keys from me.

"Please, Jo, don't do this. Don't make me leave you this way, please."

I grabbed my keys as Joanne clung to me; she wouldn't let go. I dragged her from my car door to her car door. We embraced as tears still flowed heavily.

"Please, Jo, I have to go."

I opened her car door and pushed her in. I jumped in my car and sped away. Two broken hearts headed in opposite directions. I didn't know if I'd ever see her again. I missed her already; my heart ached. I felt so numb, so worthless, so bewildered.

For sixty miles to Westford I could think of nothing but Joanne. What was this magnetic force that drew me to Westford? Was it love, was it fate, or was my reason for living only a short step away?

I arrived home. Anne could immediately tell by the expression on my face that something was wrong. I had all I could do not to break into tears. I told her the happenings of the evening. Anne consoled me and said she understood what Joanne had meant to me. Anne's situation with Ken was much the same. He had been with her for over a year, facing hurdle after hurdle.

We again talked for some time, sharing many personal thoughts. The emotional level of our relationship seemed to be on the right track. I again held back in wanting to make a total commitment. I felt in time we would find out if we were compatible. We were both trying very hard to please one another, trying not to rock the boat. In many respects it was like an entirely new relationship for both of us. If anything, we were being too cautious.

The Resniks were ecstatic about our reconciliation. John had been very hard on Anne for a year. He was very vivid and outspoken on his displeasure on Anne's decision to divorce me. He said he had been praying for two years for a miracle. The Resniks were family; they were a third set of grandparents to Steve and Dave. They showed their love in so many ways, not just after the fire, but in their everyday actions.

Gene and Katie, our other neighbors, were a little unsure of the happenings. Katie said, "We figured something was going when David said, 'My Dad's moving back home.'"

But they also couldn't figure out why my car was there for three nights and Ken's car was there for four nights. Katie said, "As soon as I'd see you drive away, ten minutes later Ken's car would pull in."

In reality it was a true-life soap opera for the little town of Westford.

My excitement of moving back home and being with Anne and the kids for the first time in six weeks was overshadowed by my thoughts of Joanne and Friday night's happenings. I wondered if she was okay? Did she really quit work and fly to California? Would I ever see her again?

I also felt threatened. I had lost a sure thing with Joanne. I was no longer playing two poker hands. Now it was only Anne and me. This added more pressure to my decision to reconcile. If things didn't work out with Anne, would Joanne be there? Or had our relationship been permanently marred?

On Saturday evening, Nancy, my mother-in-law, and Annie and I started cocktails around 5:00, and the Resniks joined us at 6:00. Nancy was spending most of her time in Westford; she was having a hard time dealing with her husband's absence. The drinks were flowing freely. It felt good to be with old friends and family. I realized over the two years of my absence how much I missed certain people. Being divorced puts a strain on friends you've become attached to. It takes a special effort to stay close.

We arrived at the Sheraton Tara in Boxboro for dinner. I had requested a nice table for a special occasion. Quickly many memories of prior occasions at the Tara flashed before my eyes.

I remembered my father-in-law telling me that a waiter had intentionally changed his tip from $10 to $20 by writing over the hard copy on his American Express bill. John had brought it to the hotel's attention and the waiter was fired.

I remembered the night Anne and I spoke of the details of the divorce over dinner. I remember breaking down after dinner. I had held back tears as I ran to my car in the parking lot. I had sat on the passenger side waiting for Anne, sobbing so loudly that a passing Good Samaritan knocked on the window and said, "Are you okay, sir? Can I help?" I nodded my head that I was okay.

Everywhere I turned the memories of the past surrounded me. We ordered cocktails and the Resniks proposed a toast to Anne and me, wishing us the best of luck and welcoming me back to the neighborhood.

Nancy said, "If John were here, I know he would be so pleased."

We enjoyed our meal and $165 later we left. The cocktails helped make Sunday arrive in quick fashion. Sunday, as usual, was a workday for me. I gave Anne a kiss goodbye. She rolled over and barely acknowledged my kiss.

"I should be home around 6:00, depending upon traffic and the Ferry schedule," I said.

I got a slight groan of acknowledgement in response.

Off I headed for Martha's Vineyard. I picked up two clients, drove the 110 miles to Woods Hole, took the 40-minute ferry ride, gave a three-hour tour, returned to Falmouth, showed some more real estate and headed north. The traffic was heavy and I was running late. I swung off the expressway to pick up a few items of clothing in Weymouth. I had no keys because I had loaned my extra set to the manager. He was away for the weekend. Joanne was supposed to leave her keys under the door. That had been arranged during the hoopla on Friday evening. Joanne was always 100 percent reliable, but Friday's circumstances changed that. No keys! I couldn't get into my own apartment! I was upset but also concerned. Maybe Joanne was really gone. No note, no signs of life, just a dark and empty apartment.

40

Only 60 more miles to home. Hopefully Anne would await me with open arms. I definitely needed some emotional support and stroking. As I pulled into the yard, I noticed Ken's car was there, which surprised me. I remembered Anne had said she was seeing Ken that afternoon to pick up a sweater and a few belongings at his house, but it was now 8:00.

What was going on? My heartbeat hastened as insecure feelings of the past came racing back. As I entered the family room, Nancy was on the couch sipping her Jack Daniels and water as I had seen her and John do for years. Her slurred speech told me she was well on her way to being buzzed.

As I looked into the kitchen there was Ken pouring himself a cup of coffee. He looked up and cordially said hello. I immediately started to tremble and fill with frustration and anger. Anne was nowhere in sight.

I said to Ken, "Where's Anne?"

"She's in the living room."

I knew that they had probably been having a heavy conversation. I was pissed off. One of my new mottos was to speak up, to not to let ill feelings fester as in the past. I wanted to know what the hell was going on.

Ken knew better than to follow me into the living room. As I entered the living room I saw Anne sitting on the couch.

"What's going on here, Anne?"

Her defense mechanisms clicked in.

"You're two hours late. Where have you been?"

"I've been working!"

"Have you been with Joanne?"

"No, I've been working."

"You're mad because Ken's here, right?"

"Well, to be honest, yeah, I'm bullshit. I work my ass off for 14 hours. I come home and your mother's boozing, Ken's in the kitchen, and you're half bombed. What the hell goes here? I feel so insecure. What's going on?"

"It's not you're being two hours late that has me upset. I've been thinking since Friday. There's too much pressure in getting back together. I don't want to be in court the rest of my life, I feel guilty. I feel like I always have to explain why I left you. Your parents will make it hard. They'll never forgive me. I know how much you love them. We'll be fighting over visiting them, because I won't want to go and face them. I can never love you as much as Joanne loves you. You're so involved in your work and career. I don't want to stand in your way or hold you back. I need a man around seven days a week. I know you can't be here all the time for me. There's too much pressure. I think too much time has gone by. Two years is a long time. I love you so much, Georgie, I'm so proud of you. I don't want to hurt you anymore. I can't be the wife you want me to be. We're just not compatible. I'm so sorry, I'm so sorry." Anne sobbed uncontrollably.

My initial reaction was to disagree, but I had also changed. I learned to go with gut reactions. Everything she said made sense. I knew Anne was right. As much as it hurt, she was right. My heart, dreams, and hopes were again shattered.

I looked Anne straight in the face and said, "I agree, I'm going to call Joanne."

As I walked up the stairs my legs trembled. My mind began to spin like a carousel. What was my purpose in life, why am I alive, why all this pain and suffering? I began to realize how much Joanne had taught me about love. I struggled because my new love for her scared me. She made me realize that the real substance of love was not physical. Love was in her smile, her touch, her caring, her sensitivity to my emotional and physical needs.

I recalled how night after night she had rubbed me down with Lanolin to ease my pain and tightness. She loved me for me. She accepted me; even all my scars were part of my whole person, a part to be loved. For two years she had been a true wife to me. She encouraged me in every part of my life. Her needs were always secondary; mine were primary to her. How could I have been so blind to her unselfish love?

I realized that over the last two years with Joanne behind me I had reached personal and financial heights almost unimaginable to most people. A large part of my drive was coming from her spark that lit my fire. It now seemed so clear.

I have always enjoyed the laughter of people, and the sense of humor that I've always had grew larger with Joanne beside me. My life over the last two years had been a positive inspiration to thousands of people. I had become the symbol of persistence, survival, success, and positiveness that all people in life strive for. I realized that I had a reason for living—a reason to share my story with others with the hope that it would enrich their lives and help show them that through love and persistence they can find success and happiness.

Was Joanne really gone? I now needed her desperately. I fumbled for a piece of paper in my wallet that had her brother's phone number. I quickly realized that I had never called her at this number. As I hastily dialed the number I knew that my life hinged on the outcome of this phone call. One ring, no answer, two rings and the phone was picked up.

"Hello, Joey, is that you?"

"Yes," came her despondent answer.

"Joey, it's all over here in Westford. I'm coming home for good. I'll explain."

After a slight pause, Joanne said, 'Georgie, I'll meet you in Weymouth in one hour." Click.

Words couldn't express my feelings as I walked through the kids' room. Nighttime had again brought peace for their innocent souls. I loved them so much. A funny clown on Stephen's dresser reminded me of the night Dad brought me the clown in the hospital. He had hoped somehow the clown would help ease my pain. Down the stairs I bolted with tears racing as fast as my legs.

Anne and I embraced for the last time.

"I'm sorry things didn't work out, Anne. I'll always be your friend. Goodbye. I love you."

Sixty miles later I found my reason for living.

EPILOGUE

Over two decades have passed since the fire that tried to take my life. If you've stayed with my story this long, you're no doubt curious as to what has happened since.

First of all, I married Joanne, my reason for living, on January 30, 1982. Here is a poem she wrote for me on the first anniversary of the fire; it will give you a deeper understanding of why I valued her love so much back then and have continued to do so every hour of our life together as husband and wife.

Twas just one year ago today
God came and nearly took you away,
But he could see at thirty-one
That your life had just begun.

My life too has known much pain
Carved further in than scars can bear,
In love we met and linger still,
And through each other learned to care.

Within your warm embrace I found
A strength and kind heart
That time and worldly worries
Can never split apart.

So let us both keep to this path
And share our many miles,
Confident that in this love
We'll know both joy and smiles.

Twas just one year ago today
God came and nearly took you away,
But he could see at thirty-one
That two new lives had just begun.

My sons, Stephen and David, are now 31 and 29, respectively. They have both completed college and started careers of their own. Stephen works in credit collections and will soon be married. David shares some of my entrepreneurial bent and has started his own business. Most importantly, we remain close to each other. They both live in Eastern Massachusetts, so we can play golf together frequently, and we sometimes vacation together.

Anne married Ken and together they stayed sober for 12 years. Unfortunately, Anne went back to drinking and divorced Ken. She has since remarried and, by coincidence, now lives in New Hampshire very near where Joanne and I live. Despite all our troubles, we managed to maintain a friendly relationship throughout the years while our sons were growing up.

I left the real estate business in 1987 and since then have worked in the financial services arena, mainly focusing on the senior market and helping people meet their insurance and retirement planning needs. I find this work hugely rewarding and truly enjoy helping people make sure they are financially secure in their elder years.

Outside of work, my chief interest has continued to be The Phoenix Society. I served first as an area coordinator and then joined the board of directors. Soon after Alan Breslau retired I even served as interim executive director until a permanent leader could be put in place. I'm very proud to say that I've been one of the organization's top fundraisers over the past 20 years or so.

From the small group that Alan started in 1977, we have grown to 10,000 members consisting of burn survivors, family members, institutions, and medical professionals. Each year we host an annual World Burn Conference that draws about 600 burn survivors from all over the globe for a four-day support meeting. We have a toll-free number (1-800-888-BURN) that people can call for support, and we publish a quarterly newsletter plus books, videos and educational materials. We also have a web site where people can connect with resources and learn more about our work (www. phoenix-society.org).

Major strides in burn treatment have been made in the years since my accident, including the development of artificial skin and improved pain therapy. As a result, the need for The Phoenix Society has grown and grown as people now survive even the most terrible of fires. With a network of support in all 50 states, we are able to reach out to these individuals and their loved ones.

If my story has touched your heart, I ask that you reach out and support the many individuals who have faced the trauma of fire. Please support the much-needed work of The Phoenix Society by sending a tax-deductible donation to: The Phoenix Society for Burn Survivors, Inc., 2153 Wealthy SE, Suite 215, East Grand Rapids, MI 49506. Thank you for letting me share my story with you and thank you also for any support you can give to the burn community.

George & Joanne Pessotti, 2005

ACKNOWLEDGMENTS

To my wife, Joanne—Thank you for your unconditional love, patience, perseverance and acceptance of me physically and emotionally.

To my sons, Stephen and David—You made me your hero. You protected me and taught me that God's greatest gifts are children.

To the memory of my parents—Thank you for all your hospital visits, prayers, home-cooked meals, love and guidance.

To my sister, brothers, friends, relatives, and business associates—Your countless cards, prayers, notes and hospital visits gave me the will to survive.

To Dr. Nick O'Connor, Dr. John Mulliken, Burn Tech Cheryl LaLonde, Nurse Rosemarie Hakem, PT, OT and the entire Peter Bent Brigham Hospital (now Brigham & Women's Hospital) and staff—Thank you for saving my life.

To William MacMillan, EMT, and the Westford, MA, Fire Department—Thank you for your prompt fire-service and professional medical attention. These services prevented serious infection and saved my life and home.

To my former business partner, Dick Valentine—Thank you for your financial support, understanding, patience, and love.

To John & Kay Resnik—Thank you for comforting my ex-wife Anne and my two sons at a time of tremendous stress and worry. You made your home a loving place at a horrendous time.

To Alan Breslau, The Phoenix Society, and fellow burn survivors—Thank you for uplifting and inspiring me through your courageous stories, but most of all, thanks for giving me hope.

To Jeanne Yocum, of Tuscarora Communications, Granby, MA–Thank you for all your editing, punctuation, and organizational skills.

And finally, to God–Thank you for giving me a second chance in life. I hope my lifetime of accomplishments and philanthropy will earn me a reserved seat in Your kingdom.